BEER ACROSS TEXAS

THE BREWMASTERS
OF THE LONE STAR STATE

Lubbock ★

NORTH TEXAS

McKinney ★
Addison ★
Grapevine ★ ★ ★ Plano
Fort Worth ★ ★ ★ Dallas
Arlington

El Paso ★

WEST TEXAS

Eola ★

CENTRAL TEXAS

EAST TEXAS

Fredericksburg ★
Blanco ★ ★ Austin
Boerne ★ ★ Wimberley
New Braunfels ★
San Antonio ★

Conroe ★
Houston ★
Shiner ★

SOUTH TEXAS

★ South Padre Island

BEER ACROSS TEXAS

A GUIDE TO THE BREWS AND BREWMASTERS OF THE LONE STAR STATE

POLING | HIGHTOWER

MAVERICK PUBLISHING COMPANY

Maverick Publishing Company
P. O. Box 6355, San Antonio, Texas 78209

Library of Congress Cataloging-in-Publication Data
Poling, Travis E., 1967-
Beer across texas : a guide to the brews and brewmasters of the lone star state / Travis E. Poling, Paul W. Hightower.
     p. cm.
Includes bibliographical references and index.
ISBN 978-1-893271-51-7 (alk. paper)
   1. Micro breweries–Texas–Guidebooks. 2. Beer–Texas–Guidebooks. 3. Texas–Guidebooks. I. Hightower, Paul (Paul W.) II. Title.
   TP573.U6P65 2009
   641.6'2309764–dc22

                                                          2009020874

10 9 8 7 6 5 4 3 2

Cover, book design and electronic publishing — Nio Graphics, Inc. and Kell Creative, LLC.

CONTENTS

CHAPTER 1

THE
NEW
BREW
MICROBREWERIES, BREWPUBS AND THE CRAFT BEER REVOLUTION

Beer has overtaken wine as Americans' drink of choice, according to a recent Gallup poll. While wine ranked slightly ahead of beer in 2005, the survey shows that within three years the tables had turned, to 42 percent preferring beer, 31 percent wine and 23 percent hard liquor.

Driving the shift has been the craft beer revolution.

America's microbrewery movement has its roots with Fritz Maytag, great-grandson of the founder of the Maytag Corporation, who bought San Francisco's Anchor Brewing Company when it was about to go out of business in 1965. Maytag customized Anchor's process and products. He soon found himself teaching others the techniques of microbrewing in order to help reduce growth pressures on his own company. As consumers developed a taste for a wide variety of locally brewed beers, the number of beer-friendly retail establishments grew as well.

In the 1970s, beer was the white bread of the adult beverage world. Mass-produced and lightened versions of the pilsner style in the United States abounded from two handfuls of large brewers, though their number soon dwindled to only four major beer companies.

Somewhere along the way, people like Charlie Papazian, a nuclear engineer, stood up and said, "I'm thirsty for good beer and I'm not going to take it anymore." Thus was born the homebrewing movement. In 1978 Papazian founded the American Homebrewers Association. The number of small breweries rapidly increased in the 1990s as a wave of states legalized brewpubs.

CRAFT BREWING

Craft brewing is not so much a matter of size as it is of quality and diversity. For example, full-bodied ales had disappeared from American commercial brewing even though they were easier to make. Over time and with the help of hundreds of millions of marketing dollars, American taste buds became used to minor variations in one style: the light American lager. By the time so-called light beer began to gain popularity, most people didn't realize they were really drinking "lighter" beer. Craft brewing, on the other hand, showcased fine ingredients, big taste and a passion for individuality.

Not all craft brewers survived. Taking shortcuts to turn a profit in tough times, or poor location or bad timing, killed many early efforts to revive numerous beer styles and a general beer culture.

In Texas, the number of brewpubs surged in the years immediately following the state's legalizing of brewpubs in 1993. Most of these enterprises failed, due to overly eager brewers who couldn't handle the process or to mounting financial pressures. Some, like the Bitter End, literally went up in smoke. Fortunately for consumers, in spite of all this the knowledge base and brewing experience have largely survived within the state. Many professional Texas brewers have patchwork quilts for resumes, having brewed at and outlasted several breweries and brewpubs.

COVEY RESTAURANT & BREWERY

Craft brewers have been producing a variety of ales and lagers in Texas since the mid 1980s.

The flurry of small brewers revealed a consumer market receptive to the idea of craft beer. Two Texas businesses turned into mega-pubs, with seventy or more beers on tap and twice that number in bottles.

The first began with a man named Bob Precious. In 1985, Precious bought a neighborhood pub on the edge of Rice Village in Houston and christened it the Ginger Man, after a novel by the Irish author J. P. Donleavy. He began with a carefully selected menu of imported beers and national microbrews. He kept the Old World feel of a traditional Irish pub, with dark natural woods and live music, but the focus was always on the beer served. The number of offerings grew along with the pub's popularity until an entire cooled wall was filled with tap handles dispensing all styles of better beers.

Precious realized his pub had created a beer culture, and expansion soon followed. A Ginger Man opened in Dallas in 1992, another in Austin in 1994. Each pub followed the same formula for beer service but remained individual and local, customized to its specific location. Precious moved to New York, where he opened a Ginger Man in Manhattan. His distance from the Texas market led him to sell his three Texas pubs to Steve Schiff in 2001. Schiff changed little from the original pub concept, and opened a fourth Ginger Man in Fort Worth in 2007.

Inspired by the concept and success of Dallas's Ginger Man, Shannon Wynne and a group of partners developed their own brand of mega-pub. The Flying Saucer Draught Emporium opened in 1995 in a historic building in downtown Fort Worth. The pub was a little more modern than the Ginger Man, with an expanded wait staff and food menu, but the centerpiece was the seventy or so beers offered on a brass draught wall and a beer menu that spanned four pages. A loyalty program called the UFO Club allowed members who drank 200 different beers to earn a plate on the wall with their name and accomplishment, creating a large group of regular patrons.

The Flying Saucer was wildly successful and became a cornerstone for the Sundance Square entertainment district in downtown Fort Worth. The success quickly led to expansion, with other Texas Flying Saucers opening in Addison, Austin, Houston and San Antonio, generally in downtown locations. The Flying Saucers in Arlington and Dallas closed, but expansion continued successfully eastward across the South, with outlets in Little Rock, Arkansas; Memphis and Cordova/Nashville, Tennessee; Charlotte and Raleigh, North Carolina; and Columbia, South Carolina.

Quietly pushing craft beer's popularity have been two Texas-based grocery chains: Whole Foods, established in Austin in 1980 and now having more than 270 locations in the United States, Canada and the United Kingdom, and H-E-B's Central Market, which opened in Austin in 1994 and has since added seven more Texas locations. Both offer an upscale shopping market with natural and specialty foods and a focus on local and sustainable providers. They do not sell liquor but carry extensive selections of local beer and wine that often rival or surpass specialty retail liquor stores.

Following an economic slump at the turn of the century, Texas brewing picked up in 2004 with two openings. Rob and Amy Cartwright, longtime professional brewers and organizers of the Texas Craft Brewers Festival in Austin, opened their own brewery—Independence—and Fritz Rahr opened Rahr & Sons in Fort Worth.

Though the worldwide hops shortage of 2007–08 and the accompanying rise in grain and fuel costs have given many brewers pause, most Texas microbreweries have plans for expansion, assuring aficionados a bright future in quaffing the delights of Texas brewpubs and microbreweries. A few more breweries, brewpubs and beer bars are scheduled to open across Texas too late for inclusion in this book. We look forward to describing and updating these developments in future editions.

BREWPUB CHAINS

Shortly after brewpubs were legalized in 1993, the first national brewpub chain with a presence in Texas became the Big Horn Brewing Company, started in 1995 in the state of Washington by a brewpub and restaurant named the Ram. Big Horn Brewing expanded as far as Texas and Illinois, franchising Pacific Northwest-themed brewpubs named Humperdink's in North Texas.

Five Humperdink's were opened in Dallas and the surrounding cities. One, established in Arlington in 1995, is still open and certified as the first brewpub in Tarrant County. The Texas locations were bought from Big Horn in 2006 and reorganized as Humperdink's of Texas, keeping existing locations and themes. Three of the five North Texas locations now brew locally and independently of any national chain, making them a genuine Texas brewpub franchise.

Meanwhile, the Santa Ana, California, BJ's Brewhouse chain was opening a few locations in the Dallas suburbs. BJ's brewing typically includes a hub-and-spoke model, with one regional brewery supplying beer for several brewpubs. But due to a quirk in Texas law that prohibits such distribution across state lines, BJ's found it more economical to contract brewing for its Texas locations with Houston's Saint Arnold Brewing Company.

The Dallas area got its first brewpub in 1995.

In 2007 BJ's began a major expansion program through the Midwest and into states east of the Mississippi. In Texas, new locations were opened in the Dallas/Fort Worth area, Houston, San Antonio and Austin, with more planned.

The third national brewpub chain to enter Texas was Gordon Biersch, based in Palo Alto, California. Its only Texas location as yet is in the Dallas suburb of Plano, which in 2008 began brewing Gordon Biersch's award-winning German-style lagers.

Current Texas law prohibits in-state brewpubs from bottling and distributing their own beers. Most national brewpub locations are either not large enough to bottle themselves or are restricted by similar state laws. Gordon Biersch is unique in operating an independent microbrewery in San Jose, California, in addition to its brewpub franchise. Both its brewery and brewpubs use the same recipes. When Gordon Biersch opened its first Texas location it became the only brewpub in Texas to also have its beers on retail shelves.

CHAPTER 2

BREWING IN
NORTH
TEXAS

ARLINGTON

🍺 Humperdink's Restaurant & Brewery

700 Six Flags Dr., Arlington, TX 76011; (817) 640-8663,
http://humperdinks.com/l_arlington.php

Humperdink's started as a sports-brewpub arm of Big Horn Brewing in the Pacific Northwest. The Texas area locations were bought out in 2006 and became the independent Humperdink's of Texas franchise. Although only the Arlington and Dallas locations brew on-site, they supply the beers for the two other locations without their own brewing operations in Addison and Richardson.

The brewpub surrounding Humperdink's has a casual sports-themed bar and restaurant with a light Pacific Northwest outdoors theme. The menu is standard American restaurant fare, including burgers, specialty sandwiches and steak platters. Each location brews anywhere from six to ten beers, including seasonals, that are fairly standard brewpub fare but can occasionally be outstanding beers.

The Arlington location of Humperdink's is unique in that it became the first commercial brewpub in Tarrant County when it opened in 1995. It remains within

Humperdink's became an independent Texas brewpub in 2006.

the shadow of both the Texas Rangers Ballpark and the new Dallas Cowboys stadium. Humperdinks became an independent brewpub in 2006.

Texas and within the shadow of both the Texas Rangers Ballpark and the new Dallas Cowboys Stadium.

DALLAS

🍺 Humperdink's Restaurant & Brewery

6050 Greenville Ave., Dallas, TX 75206; (214) 368-1203, http://humperdinks.com/l_greenville.php;

2208 W. NW Hwy., Dallas, TX 75220; (214) 358-4159, http://humperdinks.com/l_nw.php

(See description under Arlington location.)

FORT WORTH

🍺 Covey Restaurant and Brewery

3010 South Hulen St., Fort Worth, TX 76109; (817) 731-7933, www.thecovey.com

Traditionally, the concept of a brewpub meant something along the lines of sports bar meets greasy kitchen meets homemade beer. One young brewer, Jamie Fulton, opened a brewpub specifically designed to change the public's perception of well-crafted beer and the menu that accompanies it.

Fulton, a longtime Texas resident, began as an amateur home brewer but ended up with degrees from Chicago's Siebel Institute and Munich's Doemens Brewing Academy and with a pocketful of world travels. He apprenticed with Joey Villareal at San Antonio's Blue Star Brewing Company for several years before taking the plunge with his own venture, the Covey Restaurant and Brewery, which opened in 2006 near Texas Christian University in Fort Worth.

When you enter, you may not see the difference between the Covey and other traditional brewpubs. The atmosphere is elegant yet comfortable, divided between a white-tablecloth formal dining area on one side and a more relaxed bar setting on the other, with the brewing operations prominently behind glass between the two. The service is less college cheerleader and more courteous and well-informed restaurant staff.

The menu is distinctive even for a restaurant, much less for a native-grown brewpub. Entrees range from buffalo filets and elk steaks to quail and rack of lamb. Always featuring a certified master chef, the pub has a

Fort Worth's Covey Restaurant & Brewery rotates its brews seasonally.

menu highly skewed to elegant creations with southwestern and wild-game inspirations, as well as more traditional brewpub fare such as burgers and wood-oven pizzas.

The beers rotate often and seasonally, focusing primarily on world styles of beer from Fulton's own recipes. From traditional European lagers and American pale ales to foreign export stouts and Belgian tripels, Fulton has shown his flexibility and brewing skills with a wide range of traditional beer styles from all over the globe.

Although still young for a business, the Covey has received accolades from local press and patrons and has won several "best of" categories from local media. The restaurant offers special monthly multi-course dinners, each designed to pair with a particular style of beer. Fulton also holds periodic beer classes, informal affairs to educate the public about his ingredients and production.

Rahr & Sons Brewing Company

701 Galveston Ave., Fort Worth, TX 76104; tours Sat. 1–3 p.m., no charge; (817) 810-9266, www.rahrbrewing.com

Rahr & Sons' advertising is usually accompanied by the tagline "The brand new beer with a 150-year history." While it may be the newest—and now only—microbrewery in the Fort Worth area, owner and brewer Frederick "Fritz" Rahr has a brewing genealogy that goes back to German immigrants in Wisconsin; with Prohibition the Rahr family switched from brewing to grain and feed, and continues in that industry.

Rahr worked for years in the railroad industry before enduring the tedium of a corporate career, but his amateur homebrewing efforts and his genes drew him into the brewing industry. With brewing studies at Chicago's Siebel Institute of Technology under his belt, Rahr opened a brewery just south of downtown Fort Worth in 2004. Rahr & Sons has had a succession of local Texas brewers—Jason Courtney, James Hudec, Fritz Rahr himself, Gavin Secchi and now J. B. Flowers. First self-distributed, Rahr signed with local distributors in 2005, freeing up much-needed time and energy to focus on brewing operations. Tony Formby joined as an equity partner in 2007, lending some financial stability and allowing for planned expansion and growth. Production is since up to 6,000 barrels annually and climbing.

Given Rahr's heritage, the original Rahr & Sons lineup of beers featured German lagers, including local favorite Ugly Pug one of the first commercial black beers in Texas. Rahr & Sons has expanded the product line with a few more traditional ales and very popular seasonal offerings, such as Bucking Bock (a strong maibock or spring beer), Summertime Wheat (a Bavarian hefeweizen or yeast beer) and Stormcloud (the first German IPA, or India pale ale). Some experimental and limited-run products are under development.

Saturday night tours sometimes draw hundreds to Rahr & Sons Brewing Company.

In its short life, this brewery has also inspired a strong local consumer loyalty with periodic pub crawls, events sponsored by the brewery and weekly brewery tours, which can number in the hundreds. Possibly unique to Rahr & Sons is a tremendously loyal fan base and body of volunteers who show up weekly to run the bottling line for little more than a few sips of free beer.

🍺 MillerCoors Brewing Company

7001 South Freeway, Fort Worth, TX 76134; (817) 551-3300, www.millerbrewing.com

Based in Milwaukee, Wisconsin, and founded more than 150 years ago, the MillerCoors Brewing Company began distributing its beer to Texas in 1907. Far from being a Texas craft brewery, MillerCoors is second in the United States only to Anheuser-Busch in total volume produced and in total sales, and is a major brewer and employer in the North Texas region.

The Fort Worth location was the eighth major brewery built by the Carling Brewing Company, an international brewery based out of the United Kingdom and Canada, which completed its new Texas expansion 1964. At the time, the Fort Worth plant had the most technologically advanced brewing system in the world. But when the new system failed to operate properly, Carling sold the facilities in 1967 to Miller Brewing. After a $12 million upgrade and removal of the experimental brewing system, Miller began producing its own brands in Fort Worth in 1969 and by 1975 was the largest brewery in Texas.

MillerCoors Brewing is now owned by the multinational parent company SABMiller PLC, the end product of a series of brewing mergers, and Canada's Molson Coors Brewing Inc. The Fort Worth location employs more than 800 people, produces more than 9 million barrels annually and is one of Miller's seven facilities in the United States. The Fort Worth brewery also does contract brews, such as Texas beers Lone Star and Pearl, and a few imports, such as Australia's Fosters.

GRAPEVINE

🍺 Uncle Buck's Brewery & Steakhouse

2501 Bass Pro Dr. #100, Grapevine, TX 76051; (214) 513-2337, www.bigbuck.com

In late 1998 and early 1999, development started on a commercial complex in Grapevine centered around Outdoor World, a new Bass Pro Shops retailer of hunting, fishing, camping and outdoors gear and equipment. Unlike most conventional outdoor equipment stores, Outdoor

World is a huge concept store, often spanning 200,000-plus square feet of enclosed retail space complete with restaurants, stocked tanks for fishing and watching, and mounted displays of native game animals—and a few imports as well.

Because of its proximity to Dallas/Fort Worth International Airport, an Embassy Suites hotel and convention center were planned in an adjoining structure. Bass Pro contacted the Big Buck Brewery in Michigan and brokered a deal for one of their brewpub restaurants to share the building complex, the first of the chain outside Michigan. The intent was to create a destination spot for vacationers and outdoor enthusiasts. By August 2000, everything was open and operational.

The restaurant is an almost over-the-top hunting-lodge-themed establishment, complete with furniture and light fixtures of horns and hooves. The menu is traditional steakhouse fare with some wild game influences thrown in for good measure. The beer is brewed on site in large tanks visible through glass, with a smaller bar or pub area upstairs overlooking the restaurant seating.

In 2005, Big Buck's chain went through a slow series of closures as the corporation sold off assets. Fortunately for the Grapevine location, Bass Pro Shops negotiated a purchase of the adjoining brewpub and restaurant and kept it open. As Uncle Buck's the establishment has kept the same rustic aspect and hunting-themed beers, including Fallow Kolsch, White Tail Hefeweizen and Uncle Buck's Scotch Ale.

LUBBOCK

🍺 Triple J Chophouse & Brew Company

1807 Buddy Holly Ave., Lubbock, TX 79401; (806) 771-6555, www.triplejchophouseandbrewco.com

One fundamental attribute that sets Texas apart from other states is its physical size. A few burgeoning metropolitan areas are spaced out with hundreds of miles and hours of highway travel between them. Crossing the state borders can mean a two-day drive.

One modern oasis in the vast tedium of space toward the New Mexico border is Lubbock, a relatively full and active population center that earned the moniker "Hub City" for its central location amid counties of cotton farms, cattle ranches and the occasional oil derrick.

Surprisingly, Lubbock is also home to a rich tradition of homebrewers. Nurtured perhaps by the presence of Texas Tech University, or perhaps by the difficulty of obtaining beers otherwise, many award-winning amateur and professional brewers have ties to Lubbock and Tech. This city of barely 250,000 people has proven quite loyal to local commercial brewing.

Lubbock's first brewpub, Hub City Brewery, opened in 1995 and enjoyed a long run as a local music spot and award-winning brewpub. When Hub City closed in 2006, a partnership of college friends jumped at the opportunity and bought the location and equipment outright. Tech alumni Joe Keller and John Sautter, along with Joe's mother, Joyce Bigham, managed to reopen the restaurant and brewing operations within a few months as the Triple J Chophouse.

Located in Lubbock's historic district, the Depot, Triple J Chophouse is one of many destinations along a strip of local bars and restaurants. The menu features traditional steakhouse fare along with Southwestern dishes and wood-oven pizzas. The environment is not as formal as in many steakhouses, with live music on weekends that ensures Triple J is still part of the social scene.

Triple J Chophouse inherited Marks Lanham, the longtime brewer at Hub City, and he continues to produce eight to ten beers at a time. Growlers and local kegs are available for fill at the brewery. Banners from awards at the Great American Beer Festival hang on the wall, a testament to the quality still produced by this small brewpub seemingly in the middle of nowhere.

MCKINNEY

🍺 Franconia Brewery

495 McKinney Pkwy., McKinney, TX 75069; tours by appointment.
(214) 405-1719, www.franconiabrewing.com

Among the newest microbreweries in Texas is one that's also been around for a while. Franconia Brewery was opened in McKinney in early 2008 by Dennis Wehrmann, formerly head brewer for the local Two Rows Restaurant & Brewery chain.

Wehrmann is a German national who came to the United States in 2003 to work at the Two Rows Addison location. He comes from a family of professional brewers; his grandfather owned a brewery in Germany, and several family members stayed in the industry. He attended Doemens Academy in Munich and graduated with a master's degree in brewing science in 1998.

Wehrmann started with German recipes handed down in his family for centuries and plans to produce four different German styles of beer for the Texas market. First will come the house beers for the regional Two Rows restaurants and other local retail accounts, with no commercial bottling operation planned at this time. Gavin Secchi, previously of the nearby Rahr & Sons Brewery, was hired as a staff brewer and was Wehrmann's first employee.

Annual production capacity of this start-up will reach 7,000 to 10,000 barrels, which would quickly make Franconia the largest microbrewer in North Texas and reflect a growth rate parallelling the recent population growth and business development of this region just north of Dallas.

Franconia brewmaster Dennis Wehrmann comes from a family of brewers in Germany.

PLANO

🍺 Gordon Biersch

7401 Lone Star Dr., Plano, TX 75024; (469) 467-0464, 222; (817) 640-8663, www.gordonbiersch.com/restaurants/index.php

Gordon Biersch was established by Dan Gordon and Dean Biersch in 1988 in California and sold eleven years later to Big River Brewing Company of Chattanooga, Tennessee. There are now 27 locations in 16 states and the District of Columbia. Gordon Biersch brews mostly German-style lagers, and includes a full contemporary restaurant menu.

CHAPTER 3

BREWING IN ★EAST TEXAS

CONROE

🍺 Southern Star Brewing Company

1207 N. FM 3083 East, Conroe, TX 77303; check for tour dates; (936) 441-2739, www.southernstarbrewery.com

Craft beer in a can is the signature of this start-up microbrewery in East Texas. By late April 2008, kegs and sixteen-ounce cans began to make their way from Conroe into Houston and East Texas stores.

In Colorado, breweries like Oskar Blues and Steamworks have proven that craft beer in a can is not an oxymoron. And Texans love canned beer on the golf course or tubing the Guadalupe River. The first beer from inside the state's Piney Woods region is Pine Belt Pale Ale, an American-style pale ale with British crystal malts and domestic hops for bittering and aroma.

Dave Fougeron, a former brewer at Saint Arnold Brewing Company in Houston and a homebrewer since 1994, when he was a student at Texas A&M University, teamed up with longtime friend Brian Hutchins to bring

a new beer to the East Texas market. Fougeron began brewing at Saint Arnold in 1998 after choosing beer making over an opportunity to be a game warden in Nevada. He later went to the parks department in the Woodlands but was lured back to Saint Arnold as head brewer. The duo is working on additional recipes, including a German altbier.

The Anheuser-Busch plant in Houston covers two million square feet.

HOUSTON

🍺 Anheuser-Busch InBev

775 Gellhorn Dr., Houston, TX 77029; (713) 675-2311, www.ab–inbev.com

Anheuser-Busch has Texas connections dating back to at least 1892, when brewer Adolphus Busch bought the original Lone Star Brewery in San Antonio and operated it for twenty years. The Anheuser-Busch eagle can still be seen prominently in the courtyard of the complex's main building, now home of the San Antonio Museum of Art.

The St. Louis–based brewing company made its play for Texas as soon as the railroads reached enough distribution points in the 1880s and remained a competitive force for decades, even as local, regional and super-regional breweries vied for the Texans' taste buds. In 1966, Anheuser-Busch opened its Houston brewery, covering a massive two million square feet, with 950 employees that send out about 250 trucks of beer a day. The brewery has a capacity of 12.5 million barrels a year. The plant makes Bud Light (the most popular beer in Texas as measured by sales volume), Budweiser, Budweiser Select, Bud Ice, Bud Dry, Michelob, Michelob Light, Michelob Ultra and Ziegenbock. For beer drinkers on a tight budget, it also brews Busch, Busch Light and Natural Light.

The Houston brewery stopped doing tours in the late 1990s, though five of the company's twelve U.S. breweries do have formal tours, including the main brewery in St. Louis and a newer one in Fort Collins, Colorado. The Anheuser-Busch–owned SeaWorld theme park may be all about sea critters and rides, but you can also see one team of the famed Budweiser Clydesdale horses in their stalls or in full regalia pulling the reproduction of an old beer wagon. Belgian beer giant InBev purchased Anheuser-Busch in 2008.

🍺 Saint Arnold Brewing Company

2522 Fairway Park Dr., Houston, TX 77092 (soon to 2000 Lyons Ave.,
Houston 77020); tours Sat. 1–3 p.m., 45-minute tours at 1 p.m., $5;
(713) 686-9494, www.saintarnold.com

Saint Arnold is the oldest craft brewery still in business in Texas. The
microbrewery shipped its first batch in June 1994 and has been expanding
to keep up ever since. The crew is small, with less than twenty people, but
it's the biggest in the state when it comes to microbrews.

With eleven brews in the line-up—including the highly sought-after
rotating small batch Divine Reserve—Saint Arnold has something for
everyone. On the lighter side is Fancy Lawnmower, a lighter kolsch-style
brew, plus Summer Pils and Texas Wheat. For those who like it on the
maltier, hoppier side, Saint Arnold releases the amber Elissa IPA and the
brown ale year round. Seasonal delights include the slightly sweet brews
Spring Bock and Oktoberfest. Saint Arnold Christmas ale is big on sweet
malt and spicy hops, while Saint Arnold Stout has more robust flavors of
coffee and chocolate.

It should be noted that the Saint Arnold Oktoberfest, traditionally a
Marzen-style lager in Germany and at most American micros, is actually
a Scottish ale that makes for a perfect fall brew to take the edge off. It pairs
well with many hearty foods served as the weather cools.

*Owner Brock Wagner enjoys a quiet moment at
Saint Arnold Brewing Company's main bar.*

If you do your homework, you'll see that brews like the Amber, Christmas and Elissa can be found in cask-conditioned form and pulled from an honest-to-goodness hand-pump beer engine at bars such as the Ginger Man. Each is a solid beer on its own, but the cask conditioning and serving method create a different taste experience without carbonation or excessive chill to interfere with the flavors.

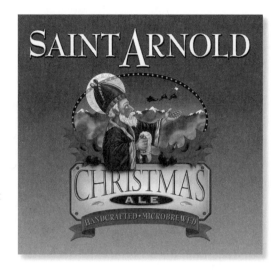

In 2008, Saint Arnold acquired a larger brewing space at 2000 Lyons Ave., the former meal preparation area for the Houston Independent School District. The three-story brick building will permit even greater production.

Brock Wagner and Kevin Bartol founded the brewery. Wagner is still there, plying a trade that was in the homebrewer's blood even as he resisted the dream, as an investment banker, for seven years after graduating from college. Wagner's three times great-grandfather immigrated from Alsace and opened Wagner's Beer Hall in San Francisco; it still exists as the Saloon after 150 years. The current Wagner grew up in both Alsace and Cincinnati, so he knew a thing or two about brewing.

Surrounded by passionate brewers, he makes a limited edition Divine Reserve brew once or more a year for enjoying right away or for cellaring. Styles for Divine Reserve have included barleywine, an Abbey-style quadruppel ale, double IPA, Scottish Wee Heavy and Russian Imperial Stout.

Saint Arnold also brews the house beers for the BJ's Restaurant & Brewery chain's Texas locations, since Texas law would require each BJ's to have its own brewing facility on site. Wagner said contract brewing makes up about 30 percent of his business.

The tours, on Saturdays, routinely draw 200 to 300 people, so get there early and plan your tasting strategy afterward. Call ahead to check on the location, due to the planned move to 2000 Lyons Ave.

TwoRows Restaurant & Brewery

2400 University, Houston, TX 77005; (713) 529-2739, www.tworows.com

Many cities around the United States are filled with long-standing and familiar brewpubs, but prior to 1993 Dallas was not one of them. When brewpubs were legalized in Texas in 1993, one of the first to open was TwoRows Restaurant & Brewery on Greenville Avenue, a location closed in 2008. Possibly unremarkable by other states' standards, TwoRows was a Texas novelty at the time: a local restaurant with good food that also brewed its own beer onsite.

Featuring a wood-fired pizza oven and a menu similar to national chain restaurants, TwoRows thrived in its location close to the campus of Southern Methodist University. Founders Mike Brotzman and Baine Brooks attribute their success to paying attention to local tastes in food and beer rather than trying to force unfamiliar styles on a young beer-consuming population.

TwoRows became so successful that the owners were able to open additional franchises in nearby Addison and close to the campus of Rice University in Houston, becoming the first brewpub in Houston. The chain runs a successful catering business and spawned a second concept in 2002 with the TwoRows Classic Grille, a similar restaurant minus the brewpub. The Houston location has kept its brewpub, while all North Texas locations are now Classic Grilles.

CHAPTER 4

BREWING IN
CENTRAL
TEXAS

AUSTIN

🍺 Draught House Pub & Brewery

4112 Medical Pkwy., Austin, TX 78756; (512) 452-6258, www.draughthouse.com

The Draught House would be an Austin favorite even if it didn't make its own beer. First of all, there are more than sixty taps of microbrews from Texas and the rest of the country and fine imports such as St. Bernardus ABT 12, the Pierre Celis–created Grottenbier and Paulaner Salvator. Add to that an unpretentious atmosphere—despite the attempt at looking like a Tudor-style pub—and you have a place that will likely become a favorite hangout.

At times a line stretches out the door into the parking lot. Once you're inside, there are large wooden tables to gather around and a biergarten in the back. On nice days, the part of the parking lot directly in front of the building becomes a welcoming impromptu biergarten, which makes it a dog-friendly establishment.

Draught House Pub & Brewery has brewed more than 40 styles of beer.

Did we mention free food? On Wednesday you'll find free pizza. On Saturdays belly up to a separate line at the bar for a generous helping of bratwurst, sauerkraut and spicy mustard on a bun. The food service begins at 5 p.m. on those days and ends when they run out.

The highlight of a Draught House visit is sampling the work of brewer and manager Josh Wilson. Sure, there are some regulars in the lineup, but Wilson likes to stretch his wings on ingredients and styles. He has brewed at least 40 styles, including a double IPA, brown, bock, hefeweizen, California common steam beer (think Anchor Steam from Anchor Brewing Co.), a variety of English styles, rye pale ale, barleywine ale, Belgian strong ale and porters that are smoked or hoppy or have an addition of vanilla.

The brewing area is tight, but Wilson manages to keep five house taps supplied year round. If you hit on a slow evening and Wilson is there, he is usually happy to show how the process works. The bartenders are knowledgeable about the house beers and the multitude of guest taps. There are no sampler trays common to brewpubs, but if you can't decide between the house beers they will gladly give you a taste before you pick your pint.

🍺 Independence Brewing Co.

3913 Todd Lane #607, Austin, TX 78744; tours first Saturday of the month, 1–3 p.m., no charge; (512) 707-0099, www.independencebrewing.com

For Rob and Amy Cartwright, independence wasn't just a Texas thing representing the fierce spirit of residents of the former republic; it also meant freedom to do what they wanted in brewing and selling their beer.

Independence started with three draught beers that soon made their way through the state in bottles. The pioneer brews by Cartwright, a former brewer at the defunct Copper Tank brewpub, are the modestly hoppy Independence Pale Ale, Bootlegger Brown with rich Belgian chocolate malt and the American-style Freestyle Wheat.

The Cartwrights have since expanded the line to include Austin Amber Beer, originally made as the house brew for the Alamo Drafthouse movie theater chain, known for serving good beer and food with its flicks. They also went big with Jasperilla Old Ale, made once a year since 2006 and aged for six months. It has a big malt character, enough hop bitterness to balance the sweetness and a powerful alcohol kick. Jasperilla ages well in the bottle, so if you see a properly stored one with an older date, don't hesitate to grab it from store shelves.

As a novelty, the amber ale gets a special label in Austin once a year right before the University of Texas at Austin and University of Oklahoma face off in their famous football rivalry. The beer's alter ego is "OU Sucks." Gimmicky? Yes, but the sentiment sure does sell some Texas beer.

On the two tours the first Saturday of every month between 1 and 3 p.m., free tickets for two or three pints are the norm. There is usually a band to let you know that though you're sitting in a warehouse parking lot in East Austin, you're still in the music capital of Texas.

🍺 Live Oak Brewing Company

3301-B East Fifth St., Austin, TX 78702; tours by appointment; (512) 385-2299, www.liveoakbrewing.com

Perhaps scarcity makes the heart grow fonder, but the beers of Live Oak Brewing Company are some of the most sought after by Texas beer enthusiasts. The microbrewery doesn't bottle and only expanded its distribution outside the immediate Austin area few years ago. But its draught beers have attained a reputation that has people eagerly awaiting their favorite seasonal to show up on tap.

Famed beer author and taster Michael Jackson declared Live Oak Pilz one of the best he'd ever had. Live Oak Hefeweizen is a mouthwatering brew that has gone from a seasonal to a year-round offering because of its

Longtime Austin brewer Julie Thompson is dedicated to the lagers that are a favorite at Live Oak Brewing Company.

popularity. And seasonals like Treehugger barleywine, Oaktoberfest and Big Bark offer something for everyone.

Chip McElroy and Brian Peters launched Live Oak in 1998 and kept the growth slow and steady. Peters eventually went on to brew at the Bitter End and now at Uncle Billy's, but McElroy kept the dream alive without succumbing to the temptation to grow too fast, the death blow for many early Texas microbreweries. The beer started trickling south to San Antonio taps when Live Oak bought a second delivery truck. Now it can be found in every major Texas city except El Paso.

They've got German brewing styles down pat with Big Bark Amber Lager, the hefe and the pilz. But interpretations of English and Americanized British styles are mighty tasty. The Liberation Ale, an IPA, and the pale ale both balance malt and hops in just the right amounts to make any hop lover happy. The hop shortage in 2007–08 finally forced a reformulation of some of the hoppy brews, but the brewers won't make anything they won't drink.

The success of the brewery has made malt deliveries seem nonstop to longtime Austin brewer Julie Thompson. The base malts come from the Czech Republic and the specialty malts come from Germany. The pilz was once 100 percent Czech Saaz hops, but the brewery is experimenting with others to deal with the scarcity. It takes about four weeks to make a lager— one of the reasons many brewpubs and microbreweries stick to the quicker ale varieties—but Thompson says McElroy will never give up the lagers that made Live Oak popular. Besides, brewing is a hot job; the employees go through a keg of pilsner a week to stay cool.

Live Oak is open for tours by appointment. They love to show folks the place and let them taste the beer from taps just steps from where it is brewed. Your best bet is to schedule a tour between 10 a.m. and 2 p.m. Monday through Thursday, but nothing is set in stone.

🍺 Lovejoy's Tap Room & Brewery

604 Neches St., Austin, TX 78701; (512) 477-1268, www.myspace.com/lovejoys

As Austin becomes more white collar and the gap between the haves and have-nots widens, the quest of some people to "Keep Austin Weird" has become quixotic and a bit of a joke to those looking in from the outside. Even some of Austin's dives have taken on the pretension of being carefully studied dives.

Lovejoy's Tap Room & Brewery has managed to avoid those pitfalls. There are no frills, and those who love the vibe at this just-off-Sixth Street locale tell me this is the real deal. Young and well-seasoned veterans of the alternative life are spotted with their tattoos and piercings side by side with beer lovers who can't wait to open up their white collars and roll up their sleeves after a long day.

A no-smoking ordinance in Austin nearly killed the establishment a few years ago; it didn't have an outdoor patio for those who like a puff of death along with their pints. But Lovejoy's has managed to hang on and keep brewing.

Longtime brewer Russell Hall left in spring 2008. The brewing is now in the hands of Todd Henry, who will keep up the tradition of aging brews in whisky barrels for added depth of flavor.

Lovejoy's beers include such favorites as Old Vixen strong ale in the winter, strong Belgian pale Beelzabubba Devil's Brew, Dennis Hopper IPA and Amber Waves of Pain. The beers seem to have improved in recent years, but the atmosphere can be very polarizing. If you're traveling with someone whose idea of a good time is wine and cheese tastings and tennis at the country club, you may be better off going solo for your beer adventure.

🍺 North by Northwest Restaurant and Brewery

10010 Capital of Texas Highway N., Austin, TX 78759; (512) 467-6969, www.nxnwbrew.com

North by Northwest is an oasis in the North Austin sprawl and traffic. Sure, it's part of a shopping center complex that typifies the suburban experience. But as soon as you enter the cool, stone interior of the brewery/restaurant you'll find a comfortable familiarity and elegance with a Texas twist.

The stone and wood exterior and interior and the high ceilings are meant as homage to the northwestern United States, where the craft

North by Northwest Restaurant and Brewery adds a Hill Country flair to the feeling of a grand lodge in the northwest, where craft brewing took hold in the 1980s.

brewing movement took off in the 1980s and 90s. The feel of a grand northwest lodge is there, but so is the Hill Country flare.

Davis Tucker started the Copper Tank Brewing Co. brewpub in Austin. While it is no longer in business, Tucker's next Austin project has thrived since it opened. Don Thompson helped install equipment and design beer recipes for North by Northwest, then left North Texas to become head brewer of the startup in Austin. Thompson was no stranger to startups. In 1982 he and his wife, Mary, started the first microbrewery in the Southwest and one of the first in the nation—Reinheitsgebot Brewing Co. in Plano. Named for the German Purity Law calling for only malt, water, yeast and hops to be used in making beer, Reinheitsgebot closed in 1990.

Mary Thompson is head of beer education at North by Northwest, which hosts regular beer classes including pairings such as chocolate and beer. Mary also writes the "Queen of Quaff" column for Southwest Brewing News.

Carrying on the brewing tradition and taking the brewpub into uncharted waters is Head Brewer Ty Phelps. Phelps, a culinary school student when he started brewing at home, interned at Bitter End Brewing and eventually landed a gig as assistant brewer to Thompson. He furthered his brewing education at the University of California at Davis and then spent time as an assistant at Real Ale Brewing Co. in Blanco. He took the head brewer title at North by Northwest in 2004 while Thompson stayed on as brewmaster. Phelps is widely credited with expanding the lineup at the brewpub and keeping it fun for customers with regular brewer's dinners.

The regular lineup includes Northern Light and Duckabish Amber. Both feature Horizon hops in varying amounts. The light beer is crisp for a hot day, while the amber has a creamier mouth feel. Pyjingo Pale Ale is fashioned after the brews ubiquitous in Northwest pubs and uses Pilsner and Caravienne malts along with Horizon, Cascade and Amarillo hops. The Okanogan Black Ale goes for a German flair, but with the addition of darker malts for a creamy brew balanced by Cascade hops. The Bavarian Hefeweizen brings wheat to the party for a refreshing German-style brew that evokes banana and clove in the cloudy concoction.

But the real stars at North by Northwest are the specialty beers, which at times are numerous. Always see what might not be on the menu or the chalkboard. On one visit, a pomegranate lambic emerged when we asked just what they might be hiding. The variety has included Kodiak IPA, a bourbon-barrel aged Whiskey River Stout, an intentionally sour Flanders red ale and other Belgian styles such as the cherry-laden Kriek, a Belgian strong pale weighing in at 8 percent alcohol by volume and a warming English-style barleywine at Christmas.

Wednesdays bring out die-hard beer enthusiasts for the tapping of a cask-conditioned beer that goes very quickly. Cask ales are typically served at cellar temperature, and have less carbonation, so the flavors really come through.

Attention to detail carries into the food and makes a fine dining experience for Austinites and visitors. The brewpub brags about its steaks, chicken and pizzas, but the dishes that have stood out on several visits over the years are the seafood offerings, as befits the northwestern theme. The beer and food can be experienced in the bar area, on beautiful patios or in the spacious dining room that still manages to feel cozy.

🍺 Uncle Billy's Brew & Que

1530 Barton Springs Rd., Austin, TX 78704; (512) 476-0100, www.unclebillysaustin.com

It's hard to get any more "Austin" than Uncle Billy's. It is family friendly, and there are big pecan trees shading a large patio and deck, quirky folk art, barbecue and fresh beer.

Uncle Billy's opened in April 2007 and quickly set the tongues of beer lovers wagging with a slate of beers true to quality and to Texas. The brewpub features six beers with at least two rotating taps of whatever pleases brewer Brian Peters, along with microbrewed beers from Austin and Houston, including Live Oak Brewing Co., where Peters was a founder in 1993.

Uncle Billy's Brew & Que is shaded by immense pecan trees.

The brewery can be seen from the bar at Uncle Billy's.

The German-style kolsch ale Back 40 Blonde, Haystack Hefeweizen, Organic Amber—this is Austin, after all—and Axe Handle Pale Ale are all regulars available by the pint or on the generous sampler along with the seasonal brews. Uncle Billy's generally keeps one tap of hoppy brew and one that celebrates the malt. On one visit, the seasonal included the Rye IPA, a brew modeled after Bear Republic's Hop Rod Rye. It included a whopping 17 percent rye malt and a mixture of Summit, Columbus, Tottenham and Spalt hops. The smoked porter uses barley malt smoked with oak and hickory wood where the barbecue is smoked.

Peters practiced his craft at Live Oak and then at the Bitter End, which closed after a fire and landlord disputes in 2005. He is quick to give tours to guests when things aren't too busy and shares his secrets with homebrewers. "I'm not secretive," Peters says. "It's really stupid to say 'I can tell what grain I'm using but not what percentage.' What the hell is that?"

While the brews aren't made with barbecue in mind as a pairing, it somehow works out that way. The clean and almost crisp blonde ale cuts through the smoke on the meat and is refreshing in the hot months. Likewise, a brew like smoked porter accentuates what is already in the brisket, chicken and ribs. Hoppier brews like the IPA and Pale Ale are good with the fiery habanero barbecue sauce offered up as an option.

The setting is ideal on Restaurant Row along Barton Springs Road just south of downtown Austin. The large patio and deck are perfect for summer evenings and early spring days. Heaters keep the chill at bay on the few cool days. When the windows are thrown open, interior seating is almost as good as being outdoors. Wave to the people who honk as they pass to let them know you can't be uptight with good barbecue and brew.

🍺 (512) Brewing Company

407 Radam Ln. F-200, Austin, TX 78745; (512) 922-8093, www.512brewing.com

Austin's newest microbrewery is another that takes its cues from pioneer Live Oak Brewing Co. Owner and brewer Kevin Brand is starting small as a keg-only business, distributing to pubs in the Austin and San Antonio areas.

Brand said he will start with "a big IPA" with Glacier hops and a pale ale that is "middle of the road" in hops and alcohol. Add to that a Belgian-style witbier—using domestic orange peel instead of imported Curacao orange—and Austinites will once again recall the days of the former Celis Brewery.

A San Antonio native and University of Texas at Austin graduate, Brand worked in California as an engineer for a decade before he followed his passion back to Austin to start a microbrewery. While he has plenty of room to grow in his South Austin facility, Brand said he will initially sell locally in keg form to bars and restaurants.

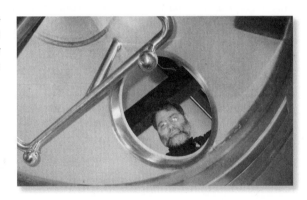

Mike Kleuber explores (512) Brewing Company during a tour.

BLANCO

🍺 Real Ale Brewing Company

231 San Saba Ct., P.O. Box 1445, Blanco, TX 78606; tasting room open Friday 2–5 p.m., tours at 4 p.m.; (512) 833-2534, www.realalebrewing.com

There was a strange charm to the original Real Ale brewery in the little town of Blanco. It was just down the street from the police station and city hall and beneath a furniture store. The ceilings were low, space was tight and the brewhouse was behind a residential-looking garage door. Somewhere in the low light, beer fermented while the brewers sipped espresso made on a machine once used by mob boss Lucky Luciano.

The brewery has since moved down the road to nicer digs with a tasting room. It may be plainer looking and a little less piecemeal, but what has been lost in charm is made up for in capacity. Real Ale can pump out way more beer from its sixty-barrel brewing system. That has allowed for better distribution of old standbys from owner and brewer Brad Farbstein, such as Brewhouse Brown, Full Moon Pale Rye Ale, Rio Blanco and Pale Ale Fireman's #4 Blonde Ale, named for a bicycle. Beer aficionados all over Texas keep bottles of the rye ale as a regular quaff in their refrigerators and eagerly await the brewery's specialty draught-only beers.

Special seasonals include organic shade-grown coffee porter made with a nice dose of fresh roasted coffee from Austin favorite Ruta Maya for the fall, the deceptively strong Belgian triple Devil's Backbone for spring and Lost Gold IPA and Roggenbier, a hefeweizen-like brew with rye malt, for summer.

Winter is a particularly fruitful harvest time, with three seasonal brews from Real Ale. Phoenix Double ESB is a powerful interpretation of the classic English extra special bitter with distinctive English crystal malt and British hops that include the Phoenix variety. Real Heavy was added in 2008, a Scottish wee heavy that weighs in at 9.7 percent alcohol by volume and is reminiscent of the Bitter End brewpub's Prescott Wee Heavy; with former Bitter End brewmaster Tim Schwartz in the brewhouse at Real Ale, this comes as no surprise.

Rounding out winter offerings is the highly collectible Sisyphus Barleywine Ale, which comes in draft and bottles and varies a little each year. Connoisseurs always buy a few extra to put in their beer cellars or in the back of a dark closet to see how the flavors change and mellow from year to year. If you're wondering, 2004 was a very good year. If a friend offers you a sip, don't turn it down.

Real Ale Brewing Company has moved into new quarters in Blanco.

Real Ale is exploring many possibilities in its new brewery and could start bottling several more of the seasonals. The brewery also contract brews the smooth and refreshing Alamo Golden Ale for Alamo Beer Co. of San Antonio.

FREDERICKSBURG

🍺 Fredericksburg Brewing Company

245 E. Main S., Fredericksburg, TX 78624; (830) 997-1646, www.yourbrewery.com

Sometimes after a day of cruising the many shops of this Hill Country town, visiting the massive Wildflower Seed Farms, the herb farm on the outskirts of the onetime German settlement and a museum or two, the traveler needs two things: a good beer and a bed. Fredericksburg Brewing Company has both.

Usually a brewpub with great beer, food and atmosphere is enough to make a beer traveler happy. Staying in one of the eleven well-appointed rooms over the brewery and not driving home is a bonus. The Bed & Brew at Fredericksburg Brewing Company in a renovated building from the 1890s make it an adult retreat that even people in nearby towns take advantage of.

Fredericksburg was already a delight for day-trippers, but the addition of the brewpub in 1994—a few months after state laws allowed the creation of combination restaurant/breweries—made it a destination for beer lovers. The owner and brewers have remained elusive during all of my visits over the last fourteen years, and the Web site hasn't been updated in three years. The beer made by Rick Green is fresh and at times fanciful.

Pioneer Porter is a consistent standout, with a deep roasted barley and a crisp finish. Other regulars include Enchanted Rock Red Ale, Not-So-Dumb Blonde and Peace Pipe Pale Ale. German tradition guides the brewing of the lagers and the ales, at 500 gallons per batch.

Specialty and seasonal brews include a Honey Cream using locally harvested honey, Haupstrasse Helles, Harper Valley IPA (Jeannie C. Riley song not included with purchase) plus, for special occasions, some big beers in alcohol, malt and hops that usually go pretty quickly. The dunkelweizen, when it makes the rotation to the tap, is a treat, especially in the fall. The Helles Keller took a gold medal at the 2008 Great American Beer Festival.

While there are plenty of German restaurants in Fredericksburg, the brewpub has something for everybody. There are German classics such as various schnitzels and sauerkraut, American standards and even Tex-

Mex plates. Even if you ate down the street during a long day of window shopping, the desserts at the brewery are a great way to draw even a non-beer drinker in your party back so you can snag another pint.

WIMBERLEY

🍺 Wimberley Brewing Company & Brew Pub

9595 Ranch Road 12, Wimberley, TX 78676; tours by appointment; (512) 847-3113, www.triomarket.com

Bruce Collie has three Super Bowl rings from his playing days with the San Francisco 49ers and the Philadelphia Eagles. Since those glory days he has settled down in Wimberley, had twelve children and taken on a restaurant. But even after all that, Collie still has his eye on the prize. This time the payoff is wowing locals and tourists to this Hill Country town with championship beers.

Along with brewer Mark Kuhlmann, Collie has created a largely undiscovered beer lovers' paradise. There is nothing on the menu to pacify the light beer drinker, just honest brews with plenty of malt and hop character.

The Fast Amber Ale has a yeasty freshness, tons of sticky lace on the glass to announce the quality of the ingredients and medium hop bitterness with touches of citrus and floral atop a slightly grassy bed. Back Rub Red Ale and Anniversary Porter stay appropriate to style and don't skimp on the ingredients. The sight of two IPAs on tap, the crispy regular IPA and the Early Bird IPA are enough to bring tears to any hophead's eyes.

Brewing days are Tuesday, Thursday and Saturday at Wimberley Brewing Company and Brew Pub.

Collie's commitment to quality brews paired with the Oregon and Alaskan brewing influences of Kuhlmann make each beer well thought out. Kuhlmann, a carpenter by trade, earned his brewing stripes as a home brewer in the Pacific Northwest after leaving the Texas Hill Country in the late 1980s. That explains the abundance of Northwest hops like Cascade and Willamette in his brews. The brewer said he is still perfecting his craft as he goes along.

Brewing days are Tuesday, Thursday and Saturday on a tiny two-barrel system in back of the steakhouse kitchen, but the brewery is preparing for a larger system as more people discover the beer and the laid-back atmosphere.

The brewpub and restaurant itself combine a rustic Hill Country setting with a touch of elegance in a sprawling rock and timber complex. If you go, make plans to spend the night after enjoying the charms of Wimberley and the tantalizing brews

CHAPTER 5

BREWING IN
SOUTH
TEXAS

BOERNE

🍺 Dodging Duck Brewhaus & Restaurant

402 River Rd., Boerne, TX 78006; (830) 248-3825, www.dodgingduck.com

When the traffic comes to a sudden stop on Highway 46 into Boerne, it's not likely to be for a traffic light. It's a safe bet that a cautious driver at the head of the line stopped for the ducks and a trail of ducklings crossing the street to the placid Cibolo Creek. One of favorite spots to cross is right in front of the Dodging Duck Brewhaus & Restaurant.

Boerne, a 30-minute drive from San Antonio on Interstate 10 West or a 45-minute drive from New Braunfels on picturesque Texas 46, may be growing in population, but the small-town feel remains. The Dodging Duck fits that scene, benefiting from locals and tourists who come for the beer and exceptional food. The menu at the Dodging Duck is diverse, with German treats like a sausage sampler platter with Central

Ducks crossing the road to Cibolo Creek gave a name to Boerne's Dodging Duck Brewhaus & Restaurant.

Texas–made links from Opa's and house-specialty beef tenderloin medallions with a spicy chimichurri sauce.

Keith Moore started the brewpub in 2002 after returning to his native Texas from years on the international brewing scene, including selling brewing equipment in Switzerland. Moore started the business with a brewer on staff but recently took over brewing himself in the tiny brewhouse behind the restaurant.

From there come sometimes great beers with names that are just, well, ducky. There's been Sir Francis Drake Porter, Quackinator Dopplebock and the Artful Dodger Barleywine, a warming brew usually on tap in December when revelers brave the cold weather for a Dickensian Christmas celebration on the streets and in the shops of the old German town. The brewpub has won World Beer Cup medals for brews such as Kill Your Bill India Pale Lager, Gunga Duck India Pale Ale, Starduck's Espresso Stout and the Marzen-style Ducktoberfest. A Bavarian hefeweizen also is a regular offering.

If Keith is around and the place isn't bustling, he may show you around the brewhouse and talk beer. If not, just kick back and relax in the converted house or on the patio overlooking the river and have a pint or two with your feathered friends.

NEW BRAUNFELS

🍺 Faust Brewing Company

Faust Hotel, 240 S. Seguin Ave., New Braunfels, TX 78130; (830) 625-7791, www.fausthotel.com

The Faust Brewing Company was launched in the renovated bar of' the historic Faust Hotel in New Braunfels in 1998. It was a much-anticipated development, for New Braunfels is the likely birthplace of brewing in Texas.

A few decent beers have come out of the Faust. But numerous brewers coming and going, difficult equipment to work with and management changes have made guesswork for thirsty locals and travelers, wondering whether they were going to find fresh-brewed beer or bottled Bud. In the early days, passable stouts and pale ales were produced by experienced brewers, but none stuck around long enough to make a mark.

After its most recent yearlong brewing hiatus, the Faust primed its taps again in spring 2008 with the Brown Ale that has been its best seller since the first day. In the recent past, beers have also included light blonde ale and a hefeweizen. Other brews were in the works.

If you're traveling, be sure to call ahead before adding this stop to your trip. New Braunfels is a charming city with plenty to see and do, and the Faust, built in 1929 just before the onset of the Great Depression, is a beautiful hotel with a quaint lobby and front entrance that draws people in. The bar area, the site of an outdoor beer biergarten before it was enclosed, also has a warm atmosphere, with a bar top of Texas pearl granite and loads of mahogany. Here's hoping the beer will one day consistently be a match for the surroundings.

SAN ANTONIO

🍺 Blue Star Brewing Company

1414 S. Alamo St., San Antonio, TX 78210; (210) 212-5506, www.bluestarbrewing.com

Joey Villarreal wasted little time in opening Blue Star Brewing Company after the Texas legislature allowed brewpubs to make and sell their own beer on site. In June 1996, a renovated warehouse space in the heart of what is now a thriving arts district became the second brewpub in San Antonio to open its taps and for years had been the only survivor.

Villarreal, whose family made a living running the legendary Sanitary Tortilla Company that supplies many of the Alamo City's Tex-Mex restaurants, found his passion for beer after opening a bar, Joey's, on North Saint Mary's Street. There he began brewing his own beer in a tiny setup on the second floor of the still-popular bar. Eleven years after the brewpub law

Blue Star Brewing has decks for outdoor dining near the San Antonio River.

Blue Star Brewing Company is housed in a renovated warehouse in what is now an arts complex.

passed that equipment is gathering dust, but his passion for great beer has never gone away.

Today Blue Star has on tap five to eight beers made by Villarreal and his assistant brewers. The brews range from a simple but thirst-quenching golden ale to the bold barley wine King William Ale, a year-round favorite. At this writing the standard golden ale was being made with lager yeast used in the classic Czech beer of Budvar, or Czechvar, as it is sold in the United States. That means the ale is not so ale-like these days, but it in no way resembles the European-style pilsner that was a regular offering at Blue Star for years. Special versions of King William Ale are made around the holidays. A recently established tradition is the King William dinner pairing various vintages of the barley wine and several variations, including aging in bourbon barrels.

Other regulars in the tap lineup include a nitro stout, amber, a pale ale and an American wheat beer. Among the occasional and seasonal offerings are a smoked dark ale, India pale ale, bock and cask-conditioned versions of the regulars pulled with an honest-to-goodness beer engine.

At Christmas, Blue Star intermittently has a hoppy brew aged with bitter and sweet orange peel dubbed Jingle Ale. The second runnings of the stronger King William Ale are usually used along with some additions. Notable offerings that could be repeated or held in secret reserve include a powerful and delicious bourbon-barrel-aged Baltic porter and a Belgian-style farmhouse ale sold under the name Biere de Bleu. Beer to go is sold in half-gallon growlers and in returnable party pigs ideal for small gatherings. Full-size kegs and pony kegs are available for larger events.

The food is burgers, pizza, fish, chicken and beef dishes, bratwurst and weinerschnitzel, salads and such standard South Texas appetizers as black bean nachos. The pork green chile is a unique and spicy offering, served by the cup or the bowl with fresh flour tortillas.

A deck for outdoor dining and sipping looks across the San Antonio River at historic homes that are part of the King William district, settled by Germans in the mid- to late 1800s. A newly constructed scenic walk runs just outside the brewpub. Across South Alamo Street is C. H. Guenther & Son's mill, known for its Pioneer and White Wings brand flour.

The city's Blue Line trolley, which costs $1 to ride, can get you from anywhere near the Alamo or convention center to a stop right outside the Blue Star Arts Complex. Or you can try the offerings of Blue Star Brewing's new bike shop, with sales and rentals for those who want to see the city in a different way. The brewery's Blue Bird Bus takes Blue Star patrons to San Antonio Spurs games in the AT&T Center, with a few fresh brews before and after the game.

Water misters keep the patio bearable in the South Texas summer, and heaters get patrons through the rare nippy eve. The inside is spacious and nonsmoking. A large back room provides space for special engagements and regularly features free events such as Big Band and the regular filming of a comedy show.

Blue Star is open for lunch, dinner and after hours Monday through Saturday. The First Friday event throughout the Southtown area where the brewery is located packs them in, so get there early and stake out a table or stool.

🍺 Freetail Brewing Co.

Northwest Military Highway and Loop 1604 West; 210-395-4974, www.freetailbrewing.com

Freetail Brewing Co. broke San Antonio's long streak as a one-brewpub town and brought fresh-made beer to the city's fast-growing and affluent north central area. The brewpub is the brainchild of economist Scott Metzger and his father, Ray Metzger, both home brewers with a passion for beer.

Named for the Mexican freetail bats found throughout South Texas, the brewpub opened its doors in late 2008. The centerpiece of the restaurant and brewery is a wood-fired brick oven for gourmet pizzas to accompany the hand crafted beer in a laid-back atmosphere.

Freetail Brewing Co. gets its name from the Mexican freetail bats of South Texas.

The full-time brewer is Jason Davis, an assistant brewer at Blue Star Brewing Company in recent years. He's responsible for keeping up to eight taps flowing with nectar including Belgian-style ales and hoppy brews that challenge the palate and don't consider compromise an answer. Davis has a long list of brewing credits to his name, including stints at Waterloo Brewing Co. and Celis Brewing Co. in Austin, where he worked with legendary Belgian brewer Pierre Celis. He also worked at the Yellow Rose Brewing Co. in San Antonio. All those brewpub and microbrewing pioneers are sadly gone, but Davis has remained steadfast in playing a role in reviving Texas beer traditions.

SHINER

🍺 Spoetzl Brewery

603 East Brewery St., Shiner, TX 77984; Tours 11 a.m.–1:30 p.m. Mon.–Fri.; Call for arrangements for groups of more than 20; (361) 594-3383, www.shiner.com

Staying in any kind of business for nearly 100 years is a difficult task. Staying in the beer business for that long was made even more difficult by Prohibition through the 1920s and, more recently, with the advent of macro-brewing dominance. For a brewery first intended to serve the needs

Copper brew kettles are features of the visitors' area in Shiner's Spoetzl Brewery.

of German and Czech immigrants to grow into an enterprise that reaches half the states in the country is a remarkable testament to perseverance.

By far the most popular Shiner beer brand made by the Spoetzl Brewery is Shiner Bock. Some beer aficionados criticize the caramel-colored brew for not being a true bock in the German style, but it has managed to find a significant following in Texas and surrounding states and recently entered the Chicago market, for a total reach of twenty-seven states, most exceptions being in the upper Midwest, New England and Hawaii.

Spoetzl Brewery was founded in 1909 in Shiner—a farming community of just over 2,000 people between San Antonio and Houston—as the Shiner Brewing Association to quench area immigrants' thirst for the beer of the Old Country. Galveston brewmaster Herman Weiss was hired as the first brewer, but by 1914 the brewery was up for lease.

German brewmaster Kosmos Spoetzl bought the brewery in 1915 after years of brewing in Canada, Europe and Egypt. He had moved to San Antonio for his health after eight years of brewing for Pyramids Brewery in Cairo. By the time he took over the Shiner brewery, there were few Texas breweries left in the state with more than a local distribution, the most notable being Lone Star and the San Antonio Brewing Association, makers of Pearl.

Spoetzl sold his beer as Old World Bavarian Draft and later changed the name to Texas Special Export. He died in 1950, but the brewery that bears his name stayed in the family until 1966. The brewery changed hands twice more but never achieved great growth. It was producing about 60,000 barrels of beer annually by 1983, but began to decline as larger brewers captured more of the market.

In 1989 the brewery's fortunes began to change. Carlos Alvarez, a San Antonio businessman who built the successful Gambrinus Co. by popularizing the Mexican import Corona, bought the brewery from a group of Texas owners. At the time, Spoetzl was down to 36,000 barrels a year, primarily Shiner Bock and Shiner Premium. By 1994, the brewery was up to 100,000 barrels. The brewhouse underwent a $40 million expansion in 1995. By 2004, the brewery had expanded and was producing about 300,000 barrels of several beers annually.

Sure, marketing had a lot to do with it, but once the brewery was on sound financial footing more beers began to roll out, expanding the line to more year-round brews and seasonals to keep the brewery relevant as thirst grew for craft beers. An attempt at a honey wheat beer was abandoned after a few years and replaced with a more straightforward hefeweizen. Shiner Kolsch, for a few years called Summer Stock, has proved a popular summer seasonal. Perhaps the most adventurous is the winter seasonal, a heartier dark brew with spicy notes in the dunkelweizen style. The brew won a silver medal in the 2008 Brewers Association World Beer Cup in the American-style Wheat Beer category.

In 2003, the brewery introduced Shiner Light. It has only 120 calories and fewer carbs than most Shiner beers, but what makes it stand out from beers held up as "light" is that it has flavor. Soft hop flavors and lightly toasted malt make for an amber lager reminiscent of certain German brews that are naturally lighter.

To countdown the brewery's milestone of 100 years in business, in 2005 Spoetzl introduced the limited Shiner 96, a well-regarded

Spoetzl Brewery's centennial in 2009 was celebrated with a special brew

SPOETZL BREWERY

German Märzen lager style typically associated with the traditional Oktoberfest in Munich. Shiner 97 was a black lager in the schwarzbier style that later became part of regular lineup under the name Shiner Black Bohemian Lager. Shiner 98 went a little lighter with a Bavarian amber. Shiner 99 in 2008 went even lighter with a helles, a bright golden brew with only 3.9 percent alcohol, Hallertau hops and both wheat and barley malts.

In spring 2008, Spoetzl made a frap for the intractable taste buds of mass-produced light beer drinkers with Shiner Spezial Leicht, or "Special Light." The beer has 99 calories—21 fewer than Shiner Light—but it didn't evoke the German traditions that most past brews did.

SOUTH PADRE ISLAND

🍺 Padre Island Brewing Company

3400 Padre Blvd., South Padre Island, TX 78597; (956) 761-9585

At the southernmost tip of Texas is a success story built on beaches and beer. Padre Island Brewing Company began with a group of shareholders who figured one of the hottest spring break locations in the country might be a good place for a restaurant and brewery. And while the typical student on holiday might not be the backbone of the business, locals and tourists alike have embraced the brewpub and kept it in business for more than a dozen years.

Mark Haggenmiller, head brewer, kitchen manager and part owner, stays inspired by the warm climes after being raised in frosty Minnesota. He also is fueled by heritage. Haggenmiller's father worked for the Gluek Brewing Company and later headed the lab at Hamm's Brewery. A great-uncle ran an oyster bar and small brewery. Three generations of brewing in the family gave the St. John's University English major more than enough incentive to dive into the business.

Working with a ten-barrel Bohemian system, Haggenmiller routinely turns out South Padre Island Blonde Ale and Speckled Trout Stout. Another regular is Tidal Wave Wheat. Among seasonal offerings are an Oktoberfest marzen beer and a maibock dubbed Cinco de Mayo Bock. Tailing Red Amber Lager and Sting Ray Scottish Ale keep things interesting among the usual taps. Haggenmiller says he is proudest of the German-style pilsner that occasionally finds its way to Padre's taps, because while it is probably the most common style of beer for Americans, a true interpretation with flavor and distinction is difficult to do right.

The atmosphere is Gulf Coast, with a metal roof, Saltillo tile and a large deck on the second floor. As the island develops, it becomes harder to find a view of the ocean or bay, but the shoreline is always close. The wait staff should be prepared with recommendations for food and beer pairings with items from seafood to burgers.

Even in the face of a hops and barley shortage expected to plague the industry for the next few years, Haggenmiller said he will not compromise: "I'm not going to make any concessions, and it's definitely going to eat into my profit."

CHAPTER 6

BREWING IN
WEST
TEXAS

EL PASO

🍺 Jaxon's Restaurants & Brewing Company

1135 Airway Blvd., El Paso, TX 79925; (915) 778-9696; 7410 Remcon Cir.,
El Paso, TX 79912; (915) 845-6557, www.jaxons.com

Established in the mid-1990s as an offshoot of Jaxon's restaurant on
North Mesa Street, Jaxon's Restaurant & Brewing Co. near the airport has
the distinction of being the fourth oldest brewpub in Texas. Given the
mortality rate of brewpubs in the early years, that's really saying something.

Jaxon's brings them in with southwestern cuisine, family-friendly dining,
televisions for sports and a lineup of beer that ranges from very light to a
hop lover's delight. The brewery has been through several brewers over the
years and an expansion to a second brewery location on El Paso's West Side.

The standard brews are Silver Star Light Ale, Borderland Lager, Cactus
Jack Amber Ale, Chihuahua Brown Ale, Black Jack Stout and Andale IPA.
The stout stands out with a smoky aroma from roasted malt. A light body
makes it refreshing even in the desert heat. The brown ale was a medalist
at the Great American Beer Festival in 1996, cementing its place on the

menu. The IPA has a light
floral hop nose and an
almost red color, with
plenty of bitterness to
go around and pair with
spicy goodies from the
kitchen. Rosa's Raspberry
Ale ventures into the
fruity side of beer and
pays tribute to the Rosa
made famous in the Marty
Robbins classic song "El
Paso."

On one visit, bartender Gordon said the IPA is a hard sell in El Paso, where macro lagers dominate even more than in other parts of Texas. But the brewery keeps cranking it out from a ten-barrel brewing system year round, because those El Pasoans who have discovered the big flavors of a hoppy beer are drinking the heck out of it. Seasonals include a Chocolate Stout, Oktoberfest and ESB.

EOLA

🍺 Eola School Restaurant, Brewery & Lodge

12119 FM 381, Eola, TX 76937; Tours by appointment; (325) 469-3314, www.eolaschool.com

Located about 25 miles east of San Angelo, the small town of Eola reached its zenith—a population of around 350—sometime after World War II. Today barely a handful of families live in town. Businesses have all but shut down or relocated to the more successful environment of San Angelo, with its military roots and university population.

But when Portland, Oregon, resident Mark Cannon wanted to move back to his Texas roots, he found the abandoned buildings of West Texas towns perfect for his plans. In 2004, Cannon bought the Eola school building, a structure dating back to 1928—and expanded with WPA funds twelve years later—that had been closed since 1983. Weather, vandals and age had done their part. Not a window was unbroken nor a door on its hinges. Ceilings were caved in and electrical wiring stripped, and the rooms were filled with trash and debris. But the town of Eola was happy to have a buyer with an interest in preserving the historic building.

It has been a monumental effort on Cannon's part to restore the school, especially considering his one-man operation and his desire to build a viable retail business on top of it. Slowly, the gymnasium was reroofed, classrooms were converted into dining halls and kitchens and the library and other rooms were fashioned for overnight stays, the beginnings of a very nontraditional bed-and-breakfast.

From the outside, the Eola School still looks like any other public primary school. Cannon's goal has been not to transform the structure but to build a new business within the school without losing the feel of the original architecture. In 2006, Cannon received a plaque from the National Park Service reflecting his building's listing in the National Register of Historic Places.

Later that year, with the science lab and the old boiler in the basement reconfigured into a small brewing operation, Cannon began brewing and serving his own beer to restaurant patrons. He started with a 60-gallon brewing system and sold 50 gallons the first day he was open. In 2006, he upgraded to a 100-gallon system, put up for sale to buy one that makes 250 gallons of beer at a time.

Cannon has also begun hosting events, such as a chili cook-offs and birthday parties, and has more plans to make the facility available for private events such as car shows and even a brewer's festival. Much more work remains, and Cannon has no plans to stop working anytime soon. The busy season comes in mid-November during the annual weekend chili cook-off. The seasonal cotton harvest drives thirsty harvest crews and cotton gin operators to line up for Windmill Pale Ale, Warlock Wheat, Eola School Chocolate Stout and Tardy Bell Brown Ale.

Despite the early successes, it's still a one-man show. The menu is nothing fancy, just traditional burgers, barbecue and chicken-fried steak. The beers are likewise fresh but not experimental. Some seasonals rotate throughout the year.

"When I make beer, I can work a twenty-hour day and then come in the next morning and clean," he said. Cannon gets a little help from a homebrewer stationed at nearby Goodfellow Air Force Base. But most of the time it's not unusual to see him working with the beer, as he puts it, "between caulking a window and flipping a burger."

Tours are available by appointment, but this is a one man-show, so availability will depend on how busy things get. You can eat, sleep and drink in the same place, but book ahead for the lodging.

Renovation began in 2004 of the abandoned school in Eola, east of San Angelo, into a restaurant, brewery and lodge.

TASTING TEXAS BEERS

Tracing styles of beer is a bit like following the family tree. There are two main branches of the beer family: lagers and ales. After that it starts to get interesting.

The difference between the two branches is the type of yeast used. Ales are made with a bottom-fermenting yeast. Most are ready to drink after a couple of weeks of fermenting at cool to warm temperatures. Lagers, however, are made with a top-fermenting yeast that came along much later in history. These beers age for more weeks in cold temperatures, a process called lagering. People tend to have preconceived notions about the characteristics of ale versus lager. Generally those notions are turned on their head when one starts exploring the world of beer.

There are five basic styles of lager. The Beer Judging Certification Program breaks them into seventeen substyles. There are about seventeen styles of broad ale, with some sixty-three substyles. Many have been added in recent years through the innovations of microbreweries and brewpubs. More, no doubt, are yet to come

What follows is a broad description of beer styles and examples you can find from Texas brewers. Most are from commercial microbreweries plus one regional brewery—Shiner—and the Big Boys with Texas plants—MillerCoors in Fort Worth and Anheuser-Busch in Houston. A few standbys at brewpubs are included, but because brewpubs are smaller and experiment more, it's best to test the lineup on the day you visit and enjoy the thrill of discovery.

LAGERS

Light American Lager

Usually crisp with very little aroma, malt or hop character. Best if served very cold.

Brewed in Texas: Lone Star Light, Shiner Spezial Leicht, Miller Light, Bud Light.

Standard American Lager

Pale golden lager with little hop aroma and a sometimes corn-like taste from cheaper adjuncts like corn syrup or rice.

 Brewed in Texas: Lone Star, Pabst Blue Ribbon, Miller High Life.

Premium American Lager

This is your basic low-hopped, crisp beer, generally made without adjuncts. Although Budweiser uses rice, it fits into this category.

 Brewed in Texas: Budweiser, Miller Genuine Draft.

Munich Helles

A medium-bodied brew that showcases soft pilsner malts and just a little hop bitterness for a clean finish.

 Brewed in Texas: Shiner 99 Helles, Rahr & Sons Blonde Lager.

Dortmunder Export

A slightly stronger version of the helles in both malt and hops that was at one time popular in the Dortmunder region of Germany but now is hard to find.

 Brewed in Texas: Gorden Biersch, Golden Export.

Pilsner

Pilsner is the progenitor of America's most popular beers, but to taste a true pilsner in classic American, German or original Bohemian style is a much different experience from tasting the light, standard and premium lagers made by the big American brewers.

This style got its start in 1842 in the town of Pilzn in what is now the Czech Republic. It was probably the world's first clear beer. The Bohemian variety is characterized by a crisp mouth feel, rich malt, Saaz hops and low-sulfate water that combine for a very soft brew. Germans later adapted the style to their own ingredients and brewing methods for brews like the popular Spaten pils. Pilsner Urquell is perhaps the best known import, but Budweiser Budvar (sold in America as Czechvar because of Anheuser-Busch's lock on the rights to the name in the United States) and Rebel also can be found.

 Brewed in Texas: Saint Arnold Summer Pils, Live Oak Pilz and at just about any brewpub that has lagers.

European Amber Lager

The two basic substyles here are Vienna Lager and the traditional Oktoberfest or Mäerzen beers. Both are characterized by rich Vienna, Munich or both malts, and by a mild to moderate hop bitterness. Vienna lager, now difficult to find in Austria, has had a resurgence in the American microbrewing scene and is revered for the toasty malts that do not sacrifice the refreshing crisp finish.

The best-known beers in this category—Negra Modelo and Dos Equis Amber—come from Mexico, where Austrian brewers began building the beer industry in the late 1800s. Oktoberfest beer, on the other hand, has flourished in its native Germany and on American shores. The style is malty, and many tend toward sweet without being cloying. Before commercial refrigeration, lagers had to be fermented and stored in cold caves. March was generally the last cool month of the year and marked the end of the brewing season, hence the Mäerzen moniker. Leftovers tended to be consumed during festivals in the fall. The Oktoberfest tradition stuck when a party was held to celebrate the marriage of a German prince around the time of the beer festivals. Colors vary from a deep gold to a dark amber.

 Brewed in Texas: Gordon Biersch Vienna Lager, Live Oak Big Bark Amber, Rahr & Sons Rahr's Red, Live Oak Oaktoberfest, Saint Arnold Oktoberfest, Rahr & Son's Oktoberfest.

Dark Lager

The three basic styles—Dark American Lager, Munich Dunkel and Schwarzbier—are as different in color as they are in taste. Dark American is usually a deep amber with a caramel malt aroma and not much hop bitterness. It is perhaps best typified in the United States by the ubiquitous Shiner Bock. Munich Dunkel tends toward brown, and has a mild sweetness and complex Munich malts that make it very rich. Many major German brewers who export to the United States make a dunkel. Schwarzbier, or black beer, is more a very dark brown than it is black and has a little sweetness, a little hoppiness, bitter chocolate notes and an underlying roasted flavor.

 Brewed in Texas: Shiner Bock (Dark American), Rahr & Sons Ugly Pug Schwarzbier, Shiner Bohemian Black Lager.

Bock

The traditional bock is a lager typically using Munich or Vienna malts for a copper color. There is a little warming from alcohol that can range from 6.3 percent by volume to 7.3 percent and very low hop bitterness.

The Germans have taken the style a long way from its origins in Eisenbeck, a city in northern Germany. Maibock, generally brewed in the spring, is more pale than traditional bock from pilsner malts used along with the Vienna. Doppelbock, or double bock, is much maltier and higher in alcohol, usually up to 10 percent. Even in U.S. brewpubs, Doppelbocks tend to end in names ending with "ator," like the classic German Ayinger Celebrator, Spaten Optimator and Paulaner Salvator. Eisbock, or ice bock, is harder to find. It tends to have more fruity flavors from the yeast, a sweet malt and a lot of alcohol, usually 9 to 14 percent, from the process of freezing Doppelbock and removing the ice crystals.

Brewed in Texas: Rahr & Sons Bucking Bock, Saint Arnold Spring Bock, Dodging Duck Brewhaus Quackinator.

ALES

English Pale Ale

Pale ales in the United Kingdom are best known by the "bitter." A standard or ordinary bitter is low in alcohol and tends to be yellow to copper in color with an assertive hop character and very rounded flavors. Special bitter, also known as Premium or Best, is a little maltier and slightly higher in alcohol than the standard variety. Extra Special, or strong bitter, is perhaps the best known of the bitter styles on American shores, where it isn't uncommon to find Fullers ESB or Old Speckled Hen on tap at an English-style pub. Even if it isn't part of the regular lineup, this is a beer at which many brewers at American brewpubs like to try their hand.

Scottish and Irish Ale

The Scottish ale style is fairly low in alcohol and bitterness but increases by degree in the form of Scottish Light, Heavy and Export. Those styles are better known under their historic designations of 60 shilling, 70 shilling and 80 shilling ale. Each has some sweetness from the malt, a dry finish and an earthiness from the smoke of burning peat used to kiln the malt, not unlike Scotch whiskey. Strong Scotch ale tends toward copper to dark brown with rich malt and nutty and smoky character. It also is bigger in alcohol, as the name implies, ranging from 6.5 to 10 percent. Irish Red Ale is amber to red with light hops, a medium body and malt. It is a little sweet, with a dry finish. Smithwick's and Murphy's Irish Red are the two most common imported versions found in Texas.

American Ale

American ale falls into three basic categories: American pale ale, amber ale and brown ale. The pale ale differs from English bitters in its use of dry hopping at the end of the brewing process. American hop varieties add a citrus character to the aroma and flavor. Amber tends to be a little darker, with more caramel malt flavor than pale. Brown ale tends toward nutty or chocolate flavors from dark roasted malts, a moderate hop charger and a somewhat dry finish.

 Brewed in Texas: Real Ale Rio Blanco Pale Ale, Southern Star Pine Belt Pale Ale, Independence Pale Ale, (512) Pale Ale, Saint Arnold Amber, Independence Austin Amber, Real Ale Brewhouse Brown and Independence Bootlegger Brown.

English Brown Ale

This is a style difficult to find in the United States, even in brewpubs. The English mild is malty, with sweet caramel, chocolate, nut and coffee flavors along with dried fruit esters from the yeast. It is generally very low in alcohol but very satisfying. Southern English Brown ale ranges from brown to black and is noted for its creaminess and sweetness. Northern English Brown is the most dominant and is typified by the nutty flavors and light caramel flavors found in Newcastle Brown Ale and Samuel Smith's Nut Brown Ale.

Porter

Porter predated stout. It is characterized by chocolate and roasty flavors like that of coffee, with a little sweetness and little hop bitterness. Fuller's London Porter is considered a Brown Porter, while U.S. examples like Sierra Nevada Porter and Rogue Mocha Porter are considered a Robust Porter. A third porter style, Baltic Porter, is very rare, particularly outside Eastern Europe. It is usually very high in alcohol, with a very full body and flavors of sweet malt, dried fruit and bold roasted flavors.

Stout

Stouts range from dry to sweet, and from low in alcohol to intoxicating. Brewed around the world, there are perhaps more variations on stout than any other major style category. Most have notes of chocolate, coffee, toffee and sometimes a little fruitiness.

Dry stout is perhaps the best known because of Guinness and Murphy's. Sweet Stout is more English in nature and is sometimes called cream or milk stout because of the use of a sweetener called lactose, the sugar found in milk. Imported examples include Mackeson's XXX Stout, St. Peter's Cream Stout and Sheaf Stout. U.S. craft brewers such as Left Hand Brewing and Samuel Adams have popular versions of the style. Oatmeal stout achieves a sweetness and silky smoothness by replacing 5 to 10 percent of the barley with oatmeal.

Foreign Extra Stout is higher in alcohol than the more common stouts, and some are very sweet. It is most typically found in tropical countries such as Jamaica, Trinidad and Sri Lanka. American Stout tends more toward the Foreign Extra with alcohol content up to 7 percent, but with more hops. The powerful Russian Imperial Stout was brewed by the English for export to Russia and was said to be favored by Catherine the Great. Lots of alcohol and lots of hops made it good for shipping long distances. Now it is mostly made in America to satisfy the growing "extreme beer" niche of craft brew lovers. The best known is North Coast Old Rasputin.

 Brewed in Texas: Saint Arnold Stout, Saint Arnold Divine Reserve No. 5 (Russian Imperial Stout, limited edition).

India Pale Ale

IPAs, so named because they were made with extra hops as a preservative to ship from England to British-occupied India for the troops in the 1800s, differ greatly in England and America. English IPAs tend toward earthy, floral and fruity hops and malts that are toasty or bready. American IPAs use hops that bring more citrus, floral and pine-like flavors to the party, while the malt leans toward a little caramel sweetness. Imperial IPAs are all about American craft-brewing attitude. They are bigger in alcohol¬—up to 10 percent—and are over the top with hop bitterness. But the moderate malt content makes it good for drinking rather than nursing.

 Brewed in Texas: Real Ale Lost Gold IPA, (512) IPA, Saint Arnold Elissa.

German Wheat Beer

Unlike American wheat beers, the Germans use a special yeast that releases complex flavors into the beer and loads of malted wheat for a very light-bodied beer that is still very creamy. The best known is Weizen or Weissbier, with its creamy white head and banana and clove notes that exist alongside faint vanilla or bubblegum flavors, depending on how it is made. The hop bitterness is very low.

Dunkelweizen has more caramel flavor and a slightly toasty character thanks to the darker Munich and Vienna malts added with the wheat malt. Weizenbock is an odd mix of a top-fermenting version of a doppelbock, traditionally a bottom-fermenting lager, but made with wheat. The powerful brew weighs in at 6.5 to 8 percent alcohol and is typically spicy and fruity but not sweet.

 Brewed in Texas: Shiner Hefeweizen.

Rye Beer

Although rye beers are hard to come by in Germany, despite their origins in Regensburg, Bavaria, they have begun to gain in popularity on the American craft beer scene. Also known as Roggenbier, they are similar to Dunkelweizen because of the darker color and the use of hefeweizen yeast, but they are made with rye malt in place of the wheat for a slight bitterness and crisp finish.

 Brewed in Texas: Real Ale Roggenbier (seasonal).

Belgian Witbeir

Soft winter wheat and added spices distinguish this once lost style from Belgium. Coriander and Curacao orange are the key spices. Brewers sometimes throw in something else for a twist. The style is very refreshing, low in hop bitterness and slightly sweet. It is best consumed fresh. After fading away in the 1950s it was revived by Pierre Celis, a Belgian brewer, in the form of Hoegaarden witbier. Celis later fell in love with Texas and started the now defunct Celis Brewing Company in Austin, with Celis White witbier as the flagship brew.

Belgian Pale Ale

This style had been around Belgium for at least 250 years when it came into its own in the 1940s. It's a little malty and a little spicy, with perhaps a citrus note or two on top of a relatively low alcohol brew. This is a session beer to sip on throughout the day, providing a big flavor without much in the way of hop bitterness.

Saison

This Belgian style is spicy with a dose of acidity, all brought together in a nearly sparkling display of small brewery craftsmanship. Expect earthiness, fruitiness and complexity with the Vienna and Munich malts that are sometimes supplemented with Belgian sugar and honey. The farmhouse brew was generally made in cool weather in Walonia, the French-speaking region of Belgium.

Biere de Garde

This is mish-mash of styles includes blonde, amber and brown varieties. What ties them together as a style is that they are aged in cold temperatures similar to the saison style, though they are sweeter, richer and without the same spiciness. They are usually consumed during the winter and range from 6 percent to a warming 8.5 percent alcohol.

Belgian Specialty Ale

Belgian Specialty is a big category that includes artisanal blonde, amber and brown beers along with blonde Trappist table beer, Trappist-monk brewed quadruples, Belgian IPAs, fruity Flanders beer, strong saisons and spiced Christmas beers hard to come by in the states. Most have bold flavors ranging from malty to hoppy and spicy to vinous. Herbs and spices are often used in the making of these brews and can be dry or sweet.

Sour Ales

Sour ales are particular to Belgium but have a German version in the form of Berliner Weisse, a wheat beer with a special bacteria that allows for a sour refreshment with low alcohol and is usually flavored with woodruff or raspberry. In Belgium, Flanders Red Ale is usually aged for at least two years in oak barrels for a sour flavor with some red wine characteristics.

Flanders Brown and Oud Bruin bring dried fruit flavors such as cherries, raisins, prunes and dates to the party along with the sourness. Blending old and young versions of the beer smooth out the rough edges a bit. Unblended lambics bring wild yeast into play for tart flavors ranging from apple to rhubarb. Fruit lambics have additions of fruit that are traditionally added about halfway through the aging process.

Raspberry (framboise), cherry (kriek) and peach (peche) are the most popular flavors, but grapes, apricot, bananas and even pineapples are sometimes added. Gueurze is harder to come by and includes no fruit. The complexity comes not only from the spontaneous fermentation but also from the traditional blending of one-, two- and three-year-old versions aged in oak before being bottled or kegged. Many bear the words "oude" or "oud" in their names, indicating "old" for the aging.

Belgian Strong Ale

This is a rich category that ranges from the Belgian Blond Ale, using a pils malt of light color, to the powerful Belgian Dark Strong Ale. The Blond is fairly sweet and a tad spicy from the hops, and generally ranges from 6 percent to 7.5 percent in alcohol by volume.

Similar in strength is the Belgian Dubbel, which originated in medieval monasteries and was revived about 150 years ago. Dubbel has a deep copper color and complex flavors such as dried fruit and is generally sweet, but it finishes on the dry side. Belgian Tripel is a deep gold with a medium body and is a staple of most Belgian breweries, including most of the famed six remaining Trappist breweries. Tripel, with a creamy head and a perfumed aroma, is high in alcohol with most of the sweetness fermented out.

Belgian Strong Golden Ale, which weighs in at up to 10.5 percent alcohol, was developed with its light golden color to compete with the growing popularity in Europe of clear pilsner lagers. While the malt is lighter here, there is still plenty of complexity, including citrus, pears, pepper and other spicy notes. Belgian Strong Dark Ale is generally 8 to 11 percent alcohol with a deep amber or dark copper color. These ales range from dry to sweet but are balanced out with a little more bitterness than the other styles of Belgian strong.

 Brewed in Texas: Real Ale Devil's Backbone (tripel, seasonal draft).

Strong Ale

The strong ale category includes Old Ale, English Barleywine and the more assertive American Barleywine.

Old Ale tends toward sweetness and is generally aged for long periods and sometimes used for blending with younger ales. English Barleywine is a strong 8 to 12 percent alcohol with big malt and dried fruit flavors, and can often be hoppier than most beers offered by a British brewery. American Barleywines are another matter altogether, the signature being a massive dose of hops and malt; they are usually offered in the winter. The alcohol is very noticeable.

 Brewed in Texas: Independence Brewing Co. Jasperilla (Old Ale), Real Ale Sisyphus (American Barleywine).

Fruit Beer

Fruit beers can be lager or ale, with the key characteristic being the addition of fruits ranging from cherries to raspberries. Some brews include apricots, elderberries, lemon, gooseberries and more esoteric fruits.

Spice, Herb or Vegetable Beer

This is a bit of a catch-all category, with a variety of established styles made with additions of chiles, chocolate, pumpkin or other flavorings. Pumpkin has become particularly popular in recent years. Some Christmas or holiday specialty brews also fall in this category.

 Brewed in Texas: Real Ale Organic Shade Grown Coffee Porter, Shiner Holiday Cheer (dunkelweizen with peach and pecan flavors).

Smoke-Flavored and Wood-Aged Beer

Rauchbier and other smoked beers are rare finds, although more brewpubs are starting to experiment with the style, which can range from smoky bacon to a drier smoked cheese flavor.

 Brewed in Texas: Southern Star Rauchbier (seasonal draft).

Specialty Beer

This is very nearly the anything-goes category, as brewers perfect their game. More than a dozen substyles might fall into this category, from Imperial Porter to a Double Brown IPA.

 Brewed in Texas: Rahr & Sons Stormcloud, Real Ale Double Wit.

LAGER/ALE HYBRIDS

Cream Ale, Blond Ale, Kölsch, American Wheat and Rye Beer

These are generally lighter styles of beer that fall in the ale category but share a smooth crispness with lagers when it comes to taste and mouthfeel.

Cream ale is a crisp and light to medium bodied beer common in American brewing. It competes with lagers and sometimes uses adjuncts such as flaked maize or sugars. Blonde Ale is a bit of a catch-all for a golden ale that ranges from extremely smooth and malty in some parts of the country to hoppier versions among microbrewers on the West Coast. For brewpubs and breweries that specialize in ales, this is often the lightest thing on the beer list.

The Kölsch style is a beer traditional to the Cologne or Köln area of Germany. It generally has a crisp, medium body and a sometimes slightly tart finish. American wheat and rye ales also fall in the hybrid category, but they tend to be a little hoppier and to have a bit more alcohol. Unlike German varieties of wheat beer, this style is much cleaner and uses yeast that won't create esters, such as banana and clove.

Rye beer has only recently begun a resurgence, with its slightly spicy character and rye grains used in moderation.

 Brewed in Texas: Real Ale Fireman's #4 Blonde Ale, Shiner Kölsch, Saint Arnold Fancy Lawnmower, Saint Arnold Texas Wheat, Independence Freestyle Wheat, Real Ale Full Moon Pale Rye Ale.

Altbier and California Common

Altbier has its origins in Dusseldorf, Germany, but also is traditional in parts of northern Germany. There is an assertive hop bitterness and dry finish. Although most altbiers are made as ales, they are fermented at cool temperatures and lagered for a lager-like character. California common, like altbier, uses a lager yeast and ferments in the usually cool temperatures of San Francisco, where the style was born at Anchor Steam Brewing Co. Northern Brewer hops are the signature of this beer.

THE HERITAGE OF TEXAS BREWING

It is difficult to imagine what early Texas explorers and settlers would have gone through to get a mug of beer. Popping down to the local icehouse or saloon for a cold beer wasn't an option.

Pausing before quaffing their brew is this august group in the Boerne area in the 1880s.

Origins of Texas Brewing, 1840–83

The first Mexican settlers likely drank a corn-based brew, letting wild yeasts convert the sugars in the grain into alcohol. Sometimes called *chichi*, it was usually made for special occasions and drunk quickly since it spoiled in the heat. Another drink called *pulche*, sometimes still consumed in Mexico, could also have been available in parts of South Texas. The thick, slimy, fermented cactus drink was made by a method that is best not explained. The next wave of settlers, the Texians, were largely from Tennessee and probably preferred a crock of whiskey that could be made in home distilleries.

In the eastern states, English settlers and their descendants were making ales in the early 1800s. Any beer that made it to Texas wasn't local, but rather a barrel of warm ale from back east that came on a wagon.

A rash of German immigration in the mid-1800s brought German brewing methods and the tradition of lagers, which ferment more slowly and at colder temperatures than ales. Germans arriving in Texas found no beer to their liking, so they began making their own. To this day, most Texas beer doesn't have a twang or a drawl; it has a decidedly German accent, with a little Czech, Austrian and Polish thrown in.

In Texas German immigrants found pure water, rich land for growing grain and the ability to obtain European hops by freight wagon. With those ingredients and a host of thirsty countrymen, Germans began brewing business as a cottage industry in Texas. Julius Rennert was perhaps the state's first commercial brewer. He settled in New Braunfels in 1846, a year after the founding of the town on the banks of the Comal and Guadalupe rivers. Rennert was the German settlement's first justice of the peace, one of its first councilmen, the first mayor pro tem and a member of the German singing society.

Census records of German settlers in Texas show few listed as brewers when they arrived. Ten years later, stonemasons, shoemakers and farmers began to show up on the books as brewers, most no doubt producing beer as a sideline since no beer manufacturers are listed in Texas records in 1850.

Rennert, also a shoemaker by some accounts, built his first brewery on the banks of the Comal River perhaps as early as 1847, and expanded in 1855. The owner of the house now on the brewery site said a few crocks and bottles remained on the basement's flagstone floor, along with markings to show how far up water came during a flood. As Rennert's trade grew, other breweries popped up in New Braunfels in the 1850s and 1860s, operated by John Schneider, Richard and August Weinert, Charles Dambmann, Karl Guenther and Mathias Esser.

Little is known about any of these early breweries, according to John Rightmire, a New Braunfels collector of bottles and brewing memorabilia. Thanks to violence in saloons, more is known about drinking establishments from the newspapers than about the breweries. "People get murdered in saloons," Rightmire told the San Antonio *Express-News*. "There's been trouble associated with alcohol since an hour after it was invented, but not many stories about breweries survived."

In Castroville, Louis Huth may have operated a brewery in the general store of George Haass from as early as the late 1840s until he moved to San Antonio in 1863. In Fredericksburg, Frederick Probst began brewing around 1857, and another brewery started in the basement of the Nimitz Hotel about 1860. A brewery in what was called the Frostown area of Houston was opened in the early 1850s by Michael and Peter Floecke. Breweries in Austin date from 1860, and City Brewery opened in 1874. Evidence of breweries in Dallas don't emerge until 1875, just before the era of big breweries.

In one of the more colorful stories about Texas brewers, the Cleburne Brewery opened in 1868 in the town of the same name. John Guepel sold his German lager for ten cents a bottle, according to Randall Scott, a novelist who is a direct descendant of Guepel. The brewery was sold to Fritz and Elijah Guffee in 1875, but, knowing nothing about beer, they brought in Mike Dixon as a partner. Dixon also apparently knew little about brewing, but he called himself a brewmaster, and soon had the enterprise in dire straights. In a gunfight over brewery finances, Dixon killed John Guffee. Elijah Guffee saw the altercation and killed Dixon with a rifle shot from across the town square. Elijah fled from a mob of townsfolk until the sheriff gave him safety. He was hanged after a short trial.

Two better-known breweries in early Texas are William Menger's Western Brewery and the Kreische Brewery in La Grange. Remnants of both still exist, one as an historic hotel once linked with the brewery and the other a preserved ruin as part of a state park.

William Menger, a German immigrant to Texas, opened the Western Brewery near the Alamo less than twenty years after the historic conflict between Texians and Mexico that turned the area into a battleground. Menger's wife, the former Mary Guenther, operated a boardinghouse in Alamo Plaza while Menger and brewmaster Charles Degen made beer that sold for 50 cents a gallon. More of the operations were turned over to Degen as the Mengers concentrated on expanding the lodgings for a few cattle drovers into a full-fledged hotel.

The hotel still stands on the site in a much expanded form and hasn't lost its reputation as some of the finest historic lodgings in the city. Don't expect to find more than a few bottles of mass-produced beers in the bar

SAN ANTONIO CONSERVATION SOCIETY FOUNDATION

Charles Degan was the brewmaster for William Menger's brewery, housed in a cellar reached by a tunnel from San Antonio's elegant Menger Hotel, built in 1859.

once frequented by Rough Rider Teddy Roosevelt, but while you're there imagine the cellars that still exist below. Menger and Degen fermented and kept cold barrels of beer in cellars with three-foot thick walls. The Alamo Madre ditch flowed through, keeping it cool even in the summer. Degen took over the brewery and moved it a few blocks away in 1879, eight years after Menger's death. Western Brewery continued as Degen's Brewery until 1915, first under Charles and then his son Louis Degen. When it opened in 1879, it was considered the largest brewery in the state.

About the same time Menger and Degen were fermenting wort in San Antonio, stonemason Heinrich Kreische decided to open a brewery of his own in LaGrange. Kreische came to Texas from Saxony in 1846 and built the county jail and a courthouse before changing his occupation to brewer. In the 1870s, he built a larger brewery down the hill from his house and thrived selling the beer for take-out in the biergarten and at a dance hall he owned in town. The brewery grew to the third largest in the state by the time of his death, but was unable to survive long under the management of his widow and the changing beer business. Tours are available. The Kreische house is on a bluff above the brewery, which sits in a ravine. Included in a state park are remnants of the brewhouse, kiln and a 40-foot deep cellar where spring water was diverted for cold storage and the cold fermentation temperatures needed over many weeks to produce German lager.

By 1870, there were dozens of breweries in Texas, mostly small operations that served their beer locally. The biggest concentration could be found in the San Antonio area, Texas Hill Country towns and the fertile farmland east all the way to Houston because of the high concentration of German and Czech settlers. Most had a life cycle equal to the life of the brewer or until greener pastures of business opportunity beckoned.

Few survived what came next.

The Railroads and Pre-Prohibition, 1883–1918

By 1880, the railroads had come to Texas. As the railhead advanced and spurs were constructed, beer barons were born. In 1881 the International & Great Northern Railroad, later part of the Missouri Pacific, linked San Antonio and Austin. By providing quick access for perishable beer into new markets, such companies as Anheuser-Busch, Miller, Pabst, Stroh and Schlitz became brewing giants. With the train came other goods, and an economic boom followed. More people meant more beer was needed.

Many local brewers hung up their paddles, unable to compete on price with the major beer barons or to afford distribution beyond their own city

Five-cent drinks drew a big crowd to this Central Texas saloon in the 1890s.

or town. A few local brewers adapted, like Julius Rennert, who signed up as one of the first distributors of beer shipped from Anheuser-Busch in St. Louis into Texas and eventually stopped producing his local beer altogether. In 1876, at the height of Texas brewing, there were fifty-eight breweries in the state. By 1889 there were eight, most of them larger operations in growing city centers. One exception was the Frank Brewery in Bellville, which lasted until the beginning of Prohibition thanks to the continuity of the Frank family running the business.

But the rail also meant that local breweries that could make the investment could also send their beer off to other cities. In 1884 Adolphus Busch started his own brewery, Lone Star, in San Antonio, the next year enlarging it with his purchase of the Alamo Brewing Co. But he was challenged by a group of San Antonians who formed the San Antonio Brewing Association and purchased the short-lived J. B. Behloradsky Brewery, on the site of San Antonio Brewing. Otto Koehler, its first manager, introduced Pearl Beer in 1886; the brewery expanded and was among the largest in Texas by 1916.

Dallas had a similar emergence of a large regional brewery, the Dallas Brewing Association. It changed hands and names several times and by the time Prohibition came to Texas in 1919 was known as Dallas Brewery Inc. In Fort Worth, the Texas Brewing Company opened in 1890 with a capacity of 50,000 barrels a year and added an ice plant that made eighty tons of ice a day.

The El Paso Brewing Association was started in 1904, but without the Bohemian influence that flavored most Texas brewing. The brewery made ales, including dark porter. After Prohibition and changing hands several times, the company brought in an Austrian brewer and production switched to lagers, perhaps more fitting to the desert climes.

In East Texas, Busch and another St. Louis brewer named William Lemp invested in the 1895 founding of Galveston Brewing Company, which survived the 1900 hurricane to make it to Prohibition.

In the early 1900s, brewer Herman Weiss moved his family from San Antonio to Galveston and opened Weiss & Son Brewery in 1907. It lasted only a few years, but Weiss's move to the town of Shiner between Houston and San Antonio was to have a lasting impact. He became the first brewmaster of the Shiner Brewing Association and established its original brewery before he left for the San Antonio Brewing Association in 1914. That opened the door for Kosmos Spoetzl to move from San Antonio to Shiner and take over the brewery, on a lease with partner Ozwald Petzold. Spoetzl peddled the dark German lager to farmers and established the Spoetzl Brewery, a lasting presence that has survived even Prohibition.

From Dry to Consolidation High, 1919–1993

Reformers in Texas called the Drys finally won their nearly eighty-year battle to ban alcohol when the state legislature ratified the Eighteenth Amendment to the U.S. Constitution. Prohibition became official throughout the nation in 1919, and by mid-January the taps stopped flowing.

Most breweries were devastated and closed. Others diversified and waited out what became a fifteen-year dry spell. El Paso Brewing produced sodas and near- beer, with most of the alcohol removed, to stay alive. Dallas Brewery Inc. became the North Houston Street Grain Juice Company. Galveston Brewing produced a near-beer called Galvo, which flopped and led them to switch to making soft drinks.

San Antonio's Charles Degen didn't live to see Prohibition shut down his brewery on Blum Street, but the Drys had been active so long and were so successful in much of North Texas that he anticipated the eventuality. He had a plan. "If Prohibition comes, Germans in this state will have to form a trust and drink up all the water," Degen was reported to have said.

In New Braunfels, the birthplace of Texas brewing, the New Braunfels Brewing Company tried to protect its investment in the plant opened only four years before Prohibition with a near-beer called Busto. Signs proclaimed: "There is no beer near here, but there is near beer here." But for the still largely German population of New Braunfels, apparently this was said with a wink and a nod. Federal agents shut down the brewery in 1925

Mechanization was aiding Texas brewers by the 1900s.

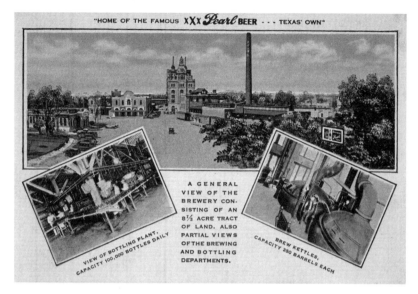

Pearl Brewery, one of the state's major brewers, was established a short distance up the San Antonio River from the Lone Star Brewery.

when they discovered the "near beer" had too much alcohol in it, and the brewery did not live to see Prohibition's repeal. The building is still there, but it has become the meat processing plant for the mail order operation of the New Braunfels Smokehouse.

Otto Koehler, CEO of the San Antonio Brewing Association, makers of Pearl Beer, also didn't live to see Prohibition. But his widow, Emma, had a plan when it came. She took over the brewery after Otto died in 1914 and is largely credited for saving the business to brew another day. It became a diversified hive selling ice, creamery products and bottled soft drinks. At one minute past midnight on September 15, 1933, the San Antonio Brewing Association was ready for the revelry that would mark the end of Prohibition. Twenty-five boxcars and more than 100 trucks left the brewery grounds "down a street lined with cheering supporters," the company history recounts.

Similar scenes were repeated at the handful of surviving breweries around the state, including those in Galveston and Fort Worth. El Paso Brewing didn't reopen until 1935, when Englishman Harry Mitchell left his bar in Juarez, Mexico, found a few partners and rebuilt the brewery. It became Harry Mitchell Brewing Co. and was fairly successful for much of the 1940s and 1950s.

With so few survivors and few if any small, local breweries trying their hand at the business, consolidation was inevitable. Oddly, one of the earliest consolidations in that period was a Texas brewery that bought out a Missouri brewer.

The San Antonio Brewing Association had great success with its Pearl Beer and changed its name to Pearl Brewing Company in 1952. Nine years later, Pearl bought the then-well-known Goetz Brewing Company of St. Joseph, Missouri, and began making Country Club Malt Liquor and the low-alcohol Goetz Pale Near Beer. Further consolidation boosted San Antonio operations with more beers, the opening of an aluminum can recycling center and a can manufacturing plant. Pabst Brewing acquired Pearl in 1985, eventually shut down its famous Milwaukee plant and moved its headquarters to San Antonio. Headquarters later moved to the Chicago area, and the Pearl Brewery was transformed into a mixed-use development that includes the third campus of the Culinary Institute of America.

In 1884 Adolphus Busch of St. Louis established the Lone Star Brewing Company in San Antonio. The logo is preserved along with its building complex, now the San Antonio Museum of Art.

Lone Star Brewery reopened after Prohibition as Champion Brewing Company with a new plant making Sabinas Beer, which later became Champion Beer. It wasn't until 1940 that brewer Peter Kreil from Munich created the formula for the first beer to actually be called Lone Star. In 1949, under the leadership of Harry Jersig, Lone Star went public. By 1960, the brewery had 651 employees and by 1965, annual sales exceeded 1 million barrels. Washington's Olympia Brewing Company bought Lone Star in 1976. It changed hands again in 1983 when Wisconsin's G. Heileman bought Olympia. Detroit-based Stroh then bought Heileman and closed the San Antonio brewery in 1996, signaling the end of San Antonio as a major brewing town. Pabst bought most of the Stroh brands, including Lone Star.

El Paso's Mitchell brewery was purchased by St. Louis brewer Falstaff for $1.5 million in 1956 and closed in 1967. Houston's Gulf Brewing Company, which started in 1933 and made Grand Prize beer, was purchased by Hamm Brewing Company in 1963 and closed in 1967, just one year after Anheuser-Busch opened its massive brewery in Houston. A Schlitz Brewing Company plant built in Longview in 1966 was gobbled up by Detroit's Stroh Brewing in 1983.

Yet the Spoetzl Brewery in Shiner is still Texas-owned and operated by Carlos Alvarez's San Antonio Gambrinus Company as a regional brewery, approaching nationwide status. Shiner beers were partly responsible for what was to come next, with brews like Shiner Bock reminding a new generation of Texans that there was something out there besides the nearly colorless lagers that had taken over the nation by the 1980s.

The Waterloo Era, 1993–2001

As recently as 1990, Texas had no brewpubs. Once homebrewing was legalized by President Carter in 1979, entrepreneurs saw the value of a growing market and a wave of brewpubs began to sprout across the United States. But even though forty-two other state alcohol boards legalized the brewpub business model, Texas still prohibited their operation.

The opposition to legalizing brewpubs is based on what has become known as the three-tier system for alcohol sales. A relic of Prohibition-era fears of monopolies within the alcohol industry, the three-tier system rigidly separates all stages of alcohol production and sales. Brewers, vintners and distillers can sell only to licensed distributors, the sole source of alcohol for retail businesses that sell to the public. Brewers are prohibited from selling directly to the public or to retail stores, and no business can own any two components of this supply chain.

Although the three-tier system is still largely intact in Texas, some major exceptions have been pushed through the legislature in the past few decades. The state wine lobby—a much more political and influential group than the brewing industry—has had the state code regulating wine and wineries filled with enough exceptions that winemakers have effectively bypassed the three-tier system on many levels. But the language of the laws has been wholly wine-centric, their benefits unavailable to the brewers of the state.

The formula for the first beer named Lone Star was created in 1940 by brewer Peter Kreil from Munich.

Public and private pressure began in the late 1980s and early 90s to legalize brewpubs in Texas, as they had been in so many other states. Legalization was repulsed for many years due to opposition from wholesalers and distributor groups, supported strongly by the traditional anti-alcohol lobby. The first crack in the armor came not from Austin but from a most unlikely player: SeaWorld.

In 1989, the SeaWorld water and marine-life theme park of San Antonio was purchased by Anheuser-Busch.

This immediately presented a legal quandary for the national brewer as, naturally, it wanted to sell its own alcoholic products in the park. However, Anheuser-Busch, having a major brewery in Houston, was now both a producer of beer within Texas and, with SeaWorld, a retailer of public sales, a situation prohibited under Texas's three-tier laws. It took less than a year for the powerful Anheuser-Busch lobby to get an exemption drafted and passed through the legislature.

Armed with this exception to the law, along with mounting pressure from businesses and tireless work from a few passionate individuals like Billy Forrester, the Texas Alcoholic Beverage Commission faced a showdown as it was held under a "sunset review"; either the TABC compromised on the brewpub proposal or proponents of the law would bring the entire TABC organization to the floor for a periodic agency-wide review and overhaul. Finally, H.B. 1425, "An Act relating to the establishment of a brewpub license," was passed by the legislature in September 1993. It was not a total victory for brewpubs, as they were prohibited from bottling their beers and selling them commercially, but it was enough to open the gates for the brewpub businesses in Texas.

Thirsty and well-funded entrepreneurs were ready to go. The years 1993 to 1998 saw a surge of brewpubs open. Some soon floundered and went bankrupt, but others prospered and established themselves for a decade or more. The first commercial brewpub was the Waterloo Brewing Company, opened by Billy Forrester in downtown Austin in the largely neglected Warehouse District. Others followed, among them the Bitter End, Copper Tank Brewing Company, Armadillo Brewing Company and Stone House Brewery. Many took advantage of Austin's Warehouse District and helped transform the area into a downtown nightlife destination.

The outright failure of many start-ups was due both to financial issues and to a zeal to brew without the talent or expertise to make salable beer. A few rebranded themselves as conventional bars and abandoned in-house brewing. But 1993 was the beginning of a "golden age" for Texas brewpubs, which began appearing in all major metropolitan areas. National chains such as BJ's Brewhouse and Humperdink's entered the Texas market, and a few native brewpubs such as Copper Tank Brewing Company and TwoRows Restaurant & Brewery were successful enough to produce branded franchises themselves.

The latter half of the 1990s saw a rise of such microbreweries as Celis Brewery and Live Oak Brewing Company in Austin, and Saint Arnold Brewing Company in Houston. The Texas economy was prospering, aided by the rise of dot-com technology. Money was not difficult to find, and many entrepreneurs turned into brewers with cash to support their pet projects.

Inevitably, this golden age was destined to end. The dot-com bubble burst around 2000, the economy contracted and the Texas brewing industry experienced a shakeout of brewpubs and small breweries. Thirty-one Texas brewpubs closed, and the number of independent microbreweries dropped to merely four. This golden age officially came to an end when Waterloo Brewing Company, the state's first brewpub, closed its doors in 2001 after eight years in business.

In Memoriam: A Directory of Departed Texas Breweries

 **North Texas**

Addison Brewing Company, Addison, 1989

Amarillo Beer and Ice Company, Amarillo

Cleburne Brewery, Cleburne, 1868–78

Dallas Brewery, Dallas, 1893–1901

Dallas Brewing Association, Dallas, 1887–89

Dallas Brewing Company, Dallas, 1889–93

Dallas Brewery Inc., Dallas, 1901–18, 1934–39

Dallas-Fort Worth Brewing Company, Dallas, 1940–51

Excelsior Weiss Beer Brewery, Dallas, 1901

First Brewery of Dallas, Dallas

Great Grains Brewing Company, Dallas, 1997–2006

Healthy Brew, Fort Worth, 2005–06 (certified organic beers)

Main Street Brewing Company, Dallas

Mingus Brewing Company, Mingus, 1908–09

Saint Andrew's Brewing Company, Dallas

Schepps Brewing, Dallas, 1934–39

Simon Mayer Brewery, Dallas, 1895–1900

Stern's Brewery, Azle

Superior Brewing Company, Fort Worth, 1933–40

Texas Beer Company, Fort Worth, 2000–02

Texas Brewing Company, Fort Worth, 1890–1918

Time Brewing, Dallas, 1939–40

Tye Dye Brewing, Dallas

W. F. Both & Company, Weatherford

Wagenhauser Brewing Association, Dallas, 1880–87

East Texas

American Brewing Association, Houston, 1893–1918

Cigar Band Brewing, Galveston

Gabel's Brewery, Houston, 1859 (?)

Galveston Brewing Company, Galveston, 1895–1918

Galveston-Houston Breweries, Galveston, 1934–55

Gulf/Grand Prize Brewing Company, Houston, 1933–63

Houston Ice & Brewing Association, Houston, 1893–1915

Houston Ice & Brewing Company, Houston, 1915–18

Southern Brewing Company, Houston, 1933–39

Theo. Hamm Brewing Company, Houston, 1963–67

Central Texas

Armadillo Brewing Company, Austin, 1994–?

Blue Ruin Brewery, Austin

Bosque Brewing Company, Waco

Capitol Brewing & Bottling, Austin, 1907

Celis Brewery, Austin, 1992–2000, Celis brand produced since 2002
  by Michigan Brewing Company

City Brewery, Austin, 1874–?

Frederick Probst Brewery, Fredericksburg, 1874–95

G. F. Giesecke & Brothers Brewery, Brenham, 1874–80

H. L. Kreisch Brewery, La Grange

Herman Frank Home Brewery, Bellville, 1882–1918

Hill Country Brewing & Bottling Company, Austin, 1993–?

Ingenhuett Brewery, Comfort, 1878–84 (?)

Kreische Brewery, La Grange, 1872–82

Lorenz Zeiss Brewery, Brenham, 1874–84

Old City Brewing Company, Austin

Steam Brewery, Austin, 1874–78

South Texas

Alamo Brewing Association, San Antonio, 1888–95

Beck's Muenchner Weiss Beer Company, San Antonio, 1907–08

J. B. Behloradsky Brewery, San Antonio, 1881–83

Bongo & Weiss Beer Bottling Works and Manufacturing Company,
  San Antonio, 1902–03

Brown Beer Brewing Company, San Antonio, 1904–05

Charles Degen Brewery, San Antonio, 1879–1911

Louis Degen Brewery, San Antonio, 1912–18

Felix Bachrach Brewery, San Antonio, 1890

Frio Brewing Company, San Antonio, 1994–99

Furstenbrau Brewing, San Antonio, New Braunfels

G. Heileman Brewing Company, San Antonio, 1983–98

Glasscock Brewing Company, Edinburg

Gustave Franke Brewery, Meyersville, 1884–1903

H. Hammer Brewery San Antonio

Lone Star Brewing Company, San Antonio, 1884–1918

Lorenz Ochs & George Aschbacher Brewery, San Antonio, 1890–1904

Michael Cellmer Brewery, Yorktown, 1878–91

New Braunfels Brewing Company, New Braunfels, 1914–18

Peter Bros. Brewery, San Antonio, 1905–10

Sabinas Brewing Company, San Antonio, 1939–40

Salado Creek Brewing Company, San Antonio

San Antonio Brewing Company, San Antonio, 1883–88

San Antonio Brewing Association, San Antonio, 1888–1918, 1933–52

Schober Ice & Brewing Company, San Antonio, 1905–18

Western Brewery, San Antonio, 1855–78

Yellow Rose Brewing Company, San Antonio, 1994–2000

West Texas

Basin Brewing, Midland

Edelweiss Brewery, Alpine, 2004–09

El Paso Brewing Association, El Paso, 1904–18

Harry Mitchell Brewing Company, El Paso, 1935–55

Old West Brewery, El Paso

Rock Bluff Brewery, San Angelo, 1878(?)–88 (?)

Sunset Brewery, El Paso

You can find more on the history of Texas breweries at www.TexasBreweries. com, an excellent Website compiled by Jeffrey Holt, and in Holt's book *Historic Texas Breweries*, available through the Website. These, along with Michael Hennech's *The Encyclopedia of Texas Breweries: Pre-Prohibition* (Ale Publishing Co., 1990), were invaluable in unearthing the past and in guiding further research by the authors.

RESOURCES FOR HOMEBREWERS

Homebrewing was born more out of necessity than out of a love of brewing. Mainstream lagers with little character or taste infested every bar and retail shelf in the country. But those who traveled in London, Germany or Belgium found more to beer than consistency and slick marketing. They discovered flavor.

Now thousands of homebrewers are making their own beer and belong to homebrew clubs. Competitions test their mettle and provide camaraderie for a journey that has more variables than wine and a trickier production process.

The Lone Star Circuit of homebrew competitions includes multiple events throughout Texas. San Antonio's Alamo City Cerveza Fest in mid-August is the newest addition to the fray. Statewide winners are picked in Houston each October at the rollicking Dixie Cup, spearheaded by the Foam Rangers. The only other competition that comes close is the Bluebonnet Brewoff just north of Dallas.

Commercial craft brewers know that diehard homebrewers are the best advocates for great beer. They are quick to speak to groups and often provide free cases and kegs of beer to urge them on.

HOMEBREW SHOPS

 **Central Texas**

Austin Homebrew Supply
7951 Burnet Road
Austin, TX 78757
(512) 300-2739
www.austinhomebrew.com

Home Brew Fetish
6533 Bandera Rd.
San Antonio, TX 78238
(210) 680-1877

Home Brew Party
15150 Nacogdoches Rd.
San Antonio, TX 78217
(210) 650-9070
www.homebrewparty.com

San Antonio Homebrew Supply
2809 N. St. Mary's Street
San Antonio, TX 78212
(210) 737-6604

St. Patrick's of Texas
1828 Fleischer Drive
Austin, TX 78728
(512) 989-9727
www.stpats.com

RESOURCES FOR HOMEBREWERS

 North Texas

Dr. Jeckyll's Beer Lab
2304 W. Park Row Drive, Suite 18
Arlington, TX 76013
(817) 274-7405

Foreman's General Store
3800 Colleyville Blvd.
Colleyville, TX 76034
(817) 281-7252
www.homebrewerysupply.com

Fort Worth Homebrew
2824 SE Loop 820
Fort Worth, TX
(817) 568-4700

Homebrew Headquarters
300 N. Coit Road, Suite 134
Richardson, TX 75080
(972) 234-4411
www.homebrewhq.com

Wichita Homebrew Supply
3274 Rogers Road
Iowa Park, TX 76367
(940) 592-5455
www.txhomebrew.com

Southeast Texas

B&S Brewers Guild
3560 NASA Parkway
Seabrook, TX 77586
(832) 225-1314
www.brewersguild.net

Brew-It-Yourself
25770 I-45 North, #107
Spring, TX 77386
(281) 367-2739
www.biy-tx.com

BrewSupplies
181 County Road 2220
Cleveland, TX 77327
(281) 432-1150
www.brewsupplies.com

DeFalco's Home Wine & Beer Supplies
8715 Stella Link
Houston, TX 77025
(713) 668-9440
www.defalcos.com

HOMEBREWING CLUBS
Active as of 2008

 Central Texas

Austin Zealots (Austin)
www.austinzealots.com

Bexar Brewers (San Antonio)
www.bexarbrewers.org

Black Star Co-op (Austin)
www.blackstar.coop

Bock 'N Ale-Ians (San Antonio)
No contact info

Brewers of Cove and Killeen (BOCK
Homebrew Club (Killeen)
www.centexbock.com

Hophead Homebrewing Fanatics
Club (Somerville
www.homebrewfanatic.com

Society of Alcoholic Professionals
(SOAP) (Helotes)
dvm2k@yahoo.com

Texas Aggie Brewing Club (TABC)
(College Station)
aayork@hotmail.com

 East Texas

East Texas Homebrewers
Association (Longview)
www.texashomebrew.com

North Texas

Cap and Hare Homebrew Club
(Fort Worth)
www.capandhare.net

Horsemen of the Hopocalypse
(Fort Worth)
www.hopocalypse.org

Knights of the Brown Bottle
(KOBB) (Arlington)
www.kobb.org

North Texas Homebrewers
Association (Plano)
www.nthba.org

Red River Brewers (Whitesboro)
sampert@texoma.net

Texoma Brews (Denison)
gtaul@webcombo.net

Three Bridges City Homebrew
(Waco)
john@wacoco-op.com

Wichita's Only Real Tasty Suds
(WORTS) (Wichita Falls)
groups.yahoo.com/group/Worts

 South Texas

Bay Area Society of Homebrewers
(BASH) (Corpus Christi)
www.beer-bash.com

The Valley HopHeads (San Benito)
fluidrive619@yahoo.com

Southeast Texas

Barley Coherent (Spring
maverickbrew@yahoo.com

Bay Area Mashtronauts
(Nassau Bay)
www.mashtronauts.com

Brew Bayou Homebrewing Club
(Clute)
www.brewbayou.org

Cane Island Alers (CIA) (Katy)
www.cialers.com

CCSD (Houston)
ccsd95@yahoo.com

Foam Rangers Homebrew Club
(Houston)
www.foamrangers.com

Friends Brewing Independently
(FBI) (Seabrook)
rsolis@hess.com

Global Brew Tribe (Vidor)
www.beertribe.com

Golden Triangle Homebrewers
Club (Vidor)
http://GTHC@beertribe.com

Houston United Group of
Zymurgists (THUGZ) (Houston)
reillygeomatics@earthlink.net

Kuykendahl Gran Brewers (KGB)
(Houston)
www.thekgb.org

West Texas

Ale-ian Society (Lubbock)
www.ale-iansociety.org

Basin Brewers (Midland)
www.basinbrewers.org

Bible Belt Brewers (Abilene)
www.biblebeltbrewers.com

Big Country Homebrewers
Association (Clyde)
bigcountryhomebrewers.
googlepages.com

HomeBrewTalk Brewers
(San Marcos)
www.homebrewtalk.com

Society for the Prevention of Beer
Blindness (Midland)
tomas13_14@hotmail.com

INDEX OF BREWERS

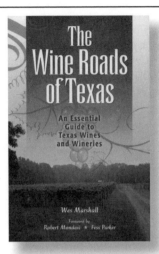
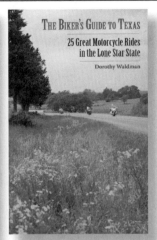
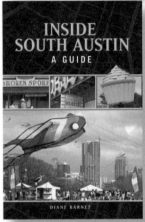
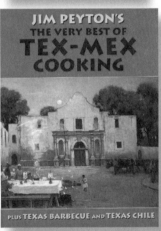

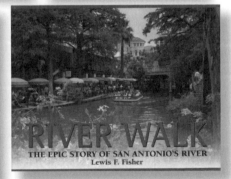